Mark Foley   Di

 D1140365

ELEMENTARY

Total English

Workbook (with key)

Longman

Contents

A

B

Vocabulary | countries and nationalities

1 **a** Complete the names of six countries. What is the letter in the centre?

A	U	S	T				A				
		B	R				N				
			R				A				
				S		?	N				
					F						D

b Complete the crossword with nationality words. There are clues in the box.

ACROSS	DOWN
6 Nicole Kidman	1 Paolo Coelho
7 Brad Pitt	2 Vladimir Putin
10 Pyrros Dimas	3 Gong Li
11 Nokia phones	4 Toyota cars
12 Roman Polanski	5 Pedro Almodóvar
	8 Leonardo da Vinci
	9 Jaguar cars

Grammar | subject pronouns and positive forms of *to be*

2 Match the questions to the answers, then match the answers to the photos.

1 Who is he?
2 Who is she?
3 What is it?
4 Who are they?

a a Rolls Royce car ☐
b Antonio Banderas ☐ D
c Brad Pitt and Jennifer Aniston ☐
d Naomi Campbell ☐

3 Complete the questions and answers with words from the box.

> Where is are British American Spain from She's He's

1 Where _____ Brad Pitt and Jennifer Aniston from? They're _____ the United States. They're _____.

2 Where _____ Antonio Banderas from? _____ from _____. He's Spanish.

3 _____ is Naomi Campbell from? _____ from Britain. She's _____.

4 Complete the questions.

What *is it*? It's a Nokia phone.

1 Where _____? He's from Russia.
2 Where _____? They're from Poland.
3 What _____? It's a Toyota car.
4 Who _____? She's Jennifer López.
5 What _____? They're students.
6 Where _____? I'm from Greece.
7 What _____? He's a student.
8 What _____? They're photos.
9 Where _____? She's from Portugal.

C

D

5 Write the full forms.

she's *she is*

1 we're We are
2 I'm I am
3 he's he is

4 they're they are
5 you're
6 it's

6 Correct the mistakes.

He's from Spain. He ~~am~~ Spanish. *is*

1 I'm Clara. I'm ~~of~~ Italy. _____
2 We're students; we is Japanese. _____
3 Where be you from? _____
4 It am a mobile phone. _____
5 Brad Pitt – who are he? _____

Pronunciation

7 Listen and underline the stress (the syllable with the strong sound).

Aus<u>tra</u>lian

1 Russian
2 German
3 Japanese

4 American
5 Chinese
6 British

Listening

8 a 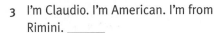 Cover the tapescript and listen to the students. Write the names on the map below.

> Maria   Misha   Claudio   John and Liz   Elda
> Jean Pierre

b Listen again and correct the mistakes.

1 I'm Maria. I'm ~~Portuguese~~. I'm from Madrid. *Spanish*

2 My name is Misha. I'm from Warsaw. I'm Russian. _____

3 I'm Claudio. I'm American. I'm from Rimini. _____

4 We're John and Liz. We're British. We're from Manchester. _____

5 My name is Elda. I'm from São Paulo. I'm Argentinian. _____

6 I'm Jean Pierre. I'm from Montreal. I'm French. _____

EXERCISE 8 TAPESCRIPT

1
A: Hello. I'm Maria. I'm Spanish. I'm from Madrid. What's your name?
B: My name is Misha. I'm from Warsaw. I'm Polish.

2 and 3
A: Hi, I'm Claudio. I'm Italian. I'm from Rimini.
B: Hi, Claudio. We're John and Liz.
C: We're British. We're from London.

4 and 5
A: Hello, my name is Elda. I'm from São Paulo. I'm Brazilian. What's your name?
B: I'm Jean Pierre. I'm from Montreal. I'm Canadian.

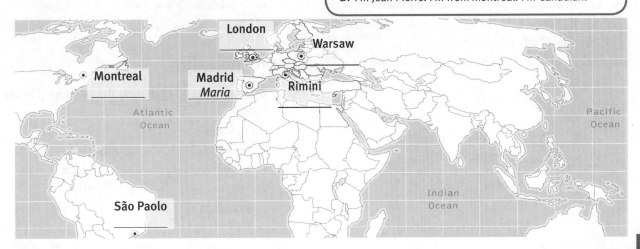

London

Warsaw

Montreal

Madrid
Maria

Rimini

Atlantic
Ocean

Pacific
Ocean

Indian
Ocean

São Paolo

1.2

Vocabulary | families

The Barone Family

Debra is Raymond's wife.
Robert is Raymond's brother.
Marie and Frank are Raymond and Robert's parents.
Ally is Raymond and Debra's daughter.
Geoffrey and Michael are Raymond and Debra's sons.
Robert is Ally's uncle.

1 **a** Read the information about the Barone family and complete the family tree.

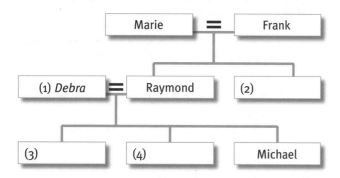

b Complete the sentences.

1 Ally is Michael's _____.
2 Michael is _____ brother.
3 Debra is _____ sister-in-law.
4 Raymond is Debra's _____.
5 Ally is Robert's _____.
6 Ally, Geoffrey and Michael are Debra's _____.
7 Michael is Robert's _____.
8 Marie is _____ mother-in-law.
9 _____ is Debra's father-in-law.
10 _____ is Ally's father.

Grammar | possessive 's

2 Make sentences using the prompts.

Jack / Hilary / husband
Jack is Hilary's husband

1 Stefan / Ana / brother
_____
2 Giorgio and Sophia / Mario / parents
_____
3 Clara / Mr and Mrs Moreno / daughter
_____
4 Vanessa / Dieter / sister
_____
5 Alejandro and Elena / Manu / children
_____
6 Victor and Serge / Halyna / sons
_____
7 Stephanie / Pierre / niece
_____

Pronunciation

3 **1.3** Listen and underline the /ʌ/ sound in the words.

grandm**o**ther

1 uncle   5 Russia
2 husband   6 nightclub
3 cousin   7 country
4 grandson

Grammar | possessive adjectives

4   **a**   Look at the picture. Match 1–4 below to the things in the picture (A–D).

1   Is this your car? – Yes, it's our car.   ☐
2   Is this your car? – No, it's his car.   ☐
3   Is this your house? – Yes, it's our house.   ☐
4   Is this your house? – No, it's her house.   ☐

b   Underline the correct word in italics.

1   A is *my/their* house.
2   B is *her/their* car.
3   C is *her/his* car.
4   D is *her/his* house.

5   Correct the underlined mistakes. Use possessive adjectives.

Is <u>you</u> sister married? *your*

1   Are <u>he</u> brothers and sisters Canadian? _____
2   Is <u>she</u> house in New York? _____
3   This is <u>I</u> dictionary. _____
4   Jennifer is <u>we</u> cousin. _____
5   Is this <u>you</u> mobile phone? _____

Grammar | *to be* (questions)

6   Match the questions to the answers.

1   Is Elizabeth your sister?   a   Yes, I am.
2   Are Sally and John your   b   Yes, we are.
    parents?   c   No, they're
3   Is David your brother?   my sisters.
4   Are you a student?   d   Yes, she is.
5   Are we in the   e   Yes, they are.
    elementary class?   f   No, he's my
6   Are Elizabeth and Marie   boyfriend.
    your cousins?

Listening ✳

7   **1.4** Cover the tapescript. Listen and answer the questions.

Where is Amanda from? *She's from Melbourne.*

1   Is Amanda Australian?
    _____
2   Where are her parents from?
    _____
3   What is her husband's name?
    _____
4   Is he from the United States?
    _____
5   Where are his parents from?
    _____
6   Where is their house?
    _____
7   Is Amanda a student?
    _____

EXERCISE 7 TAPESCRIPT

Hi. I'm Amanda. I'm from Melbourne, in Australia. I'm Australian but my parents are from Greece, they're Greek. John is my husband. He's Australian but his parents are from the United States. Our house is in Sydney. I'm a student at Sydney University.

Vocabulary | jobs (Vocabulary Bank, p84)

1 Look at the pictures and the letters. Write the job words. Some jobs are two words.

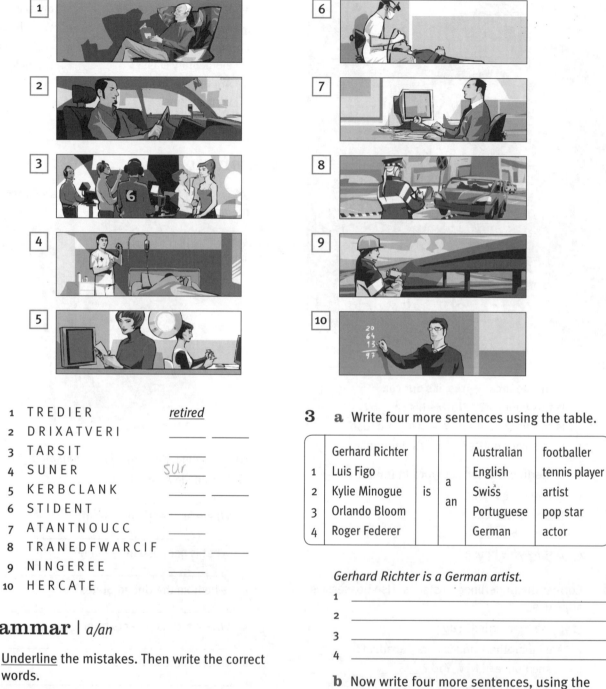

1	T R E D I E R
2	D R I X A T V E R I
3	T A R S I T
4	S U N E R
5	K E R B C L A N K
6	S T I D E N T
7	A T A N T N O U C C
8	T R A N E D F W A R C I F
9	N I N G E R E E
10	H E R C A T E

1 TREDIER — *retired*
2 DRIXATVERI — _____ _____
3 TARSIT — _____
4 SUNER — *sur_____*
5 KERBCLANK — _____ _____
6 STIDENT — _____
7 ATANTNOUCC — _____
8 TRANEDFWARCIF — _____ _____
9 NINGEREE — _____
10 HERCATE — _____

Grammar | a/an

2 <u>Underline</u> the mistakes. Then write the correct words.

My brother <u>is student</u>.   *a student*
Sam's <u>a</u> electrician.   *an electrician*

1 My cousin Julia's an nurse. _____
2 My grandfather is a retired. _____
3 Pablo's engineer in Brussels. _____
4 My father's a unemployed. _____
5 Lucia's friend is lawyer in New York. _____
6 I'm an clerk in my uncle's bank. _____

3   **a** Write four more sentences using the table.

1	Gerhard Richter Luis Figo	is	a an	Australian	footballer
2	Kylie Minogue			English Swiss	tennis player artist
3	Orlando Bloom			Portuguese	pop star
4	Roger Federer			German	actor

Gerhard Richter is a German artist.

1 _____
2 _____
3 _____
4 _____

b Now write four more sentences, using the jobs in Ex. 3a and/or these jobs.

architect   doctor   film star   police officer
journalist

1 _____
2 _____
3 _____
4 _____

Grammar | *to be* (negative)

4   **a** Put the words in the correct order to make sentences. Use contracted forms.

not Lukasc married Susanna are and

Lukasc and Susanna aren' t married.

1 My 20, Cedar Drive not address is

_____

2 retired grandparents are My not

_____

3 little beautiful is sister My not

_____

4 from not Colombia is Esther

_____

5 doctor not is My nephew a

_____

6 Canadian not My are parents

_____

b Rewrite the sentences from Ex. 4a in the affirmative.

Lukasc and Susanna are married.

1 _____
2 _____
3 _____
4 _____
5 _____
6 _____

Reading and writing

5   **a** Read about Rainer and complete the gaps with words from the box.

> email   from   manager   married   mobile
> ~~name~~   old   phone

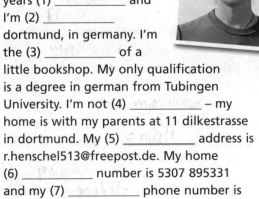

Hello, my *name* is rainer henschel. I'm twenty-four years (1) _o l d_ and I'm (2) _____ dortmund, in germany. I'm the (3) _ma_____ of a little bookshop. My only qualification is a degree in german from Tubingen University. I'm not (4) _____ – my home is with my parents at 11 dilkestrasse in dortmund. My (5) _email_ address is r.henschel513@freepost.de. My home (6) _phone_ number is 5307 895331 and my (7) _mobile_ phone number is 07632 116789.

b In English, we use capital letters at the beginning of names of people and places. Find six more mistakes with capital letters in the text and correct them here. (Look at the Writing Bank on page 145 of your Students' Book to help you.)

rainer = Rainer

1 _____   4 _____
2 _____   5 _____
3 _____   6 _____

6   **a** Read the text in Ex. 5a again and complete the form for Rainer.

Perfect Partners on the Net

1. First name: _____
2. Surname: _____
3. Age: _____
4. Place of origin: _____
5. Nationality: _____
6. Married ☐   Single ☐
7. Address: _____
8. Email address: _____
9. Home telephone number: _____
10. Mobile telephone number: _____
11. Occupation: _____
12. Qualifications: _____

b Complete this form for you.

Perfect Partners on the Net

1. First name: _____
2. Surname: _____
3. Age: _____
4. Place of origin: _____
5. Nationality: _____
6. Married ☐   Single ☐
7. Address: _____
8. Email address: _____
9. Home telephone number: _____
10. Mobile telephone number: _____
11. Occupation: _____
12. Qualifications: _____

Grammar | Present Simple: *I/you/we*

1 **a** Danny is 32. He is the manager of a holiday hotel in the Caribbean. Read the notes about Danny's daily routine.

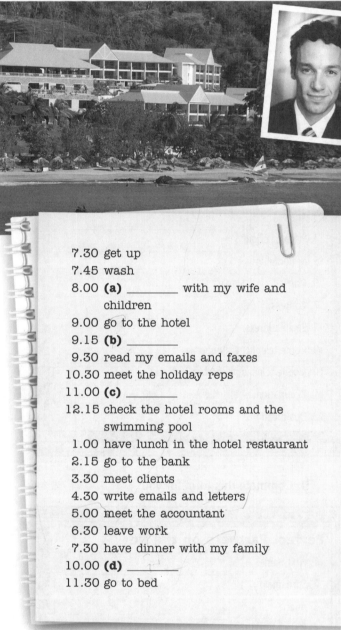

7.30 get up
7.45 wash
8.00 **(a)** _____ with my wife and children
9.00 go to the hotel
9.15 **(b)** _____
9.30 read my emails and faxes
10.30 meet the holiday reps
11.00 **(c)** _____
12.15 check the hotel rooms and the swimming pool
1.00 have lunch in the hotel restaurant
2.15 go to the bank
3.30 meet clients
4.30 write emails and letters
5.00 meet the accountant
6.30 leave work
7.30 have dinner with my family
10.00 **(d)** _____
11.30 go to bed

You are Danny. Answer the questions.

When do you get up?
I get up at half past seven.

1 What do you do at quarter to eight?
_____

2 When do you go to work?
_____

3 What do you do at quarter past twelve?
_____

4 Where do you have lunch?
_____

5 When do you have lunch?
_____

6 What do you do in the evening?
_____

7 When do you go to bed?
_____

b You are Danny. Write short answers.

Do you have breakfast at half past eight?
No, I don't.

1 Do you have breakfast in a hotel?
_____

2 Are you a hotel manager?
_____

3 Do you have a family?
_____

4 Do you have lunch in a restaurant?
_____

5 Do you leave work at six o'clock?
_____

6 Are you 32?
_____

7 Do you go to bed at eleven o'clock?
_____

c Read the questions in Ex. 1a and 1b again. Write true answers about you in your notebook.

Listening

2 **a** **2.1** Cover the tapescript. Listen and complete the notes a–d in Ex. 1a.

b Listen again and tick (✓) the things you hear. Cross (✗) the things you don't hear.

1 a) When do you start work? ☐
  b) When you start work? ☐
2 a) What do you do in the morning? ☐
  b) What are you do in the morning? ☐
3 a) We have coffee at eleven o'clock in the hotel. ☐
  b) We have coffee at eleven o'clock in the office. ☐
4 a) I go to the bank. Then I meet the hotel clients. ☐
  b) I go to the bank and I meet the hotel clients. ☐
5 a) Do you work in office? ☐
  b) Do you work in the office? ☐
6 a) At ten o'clock I watch the news on TV. ☐
  b) At ten o'clock I watch the films on TV. ☐

c Look at the tapescript on page 11 and check your answers.

EXERCISE 2 TAPESCRIPT

Interviewer: Danny. Tell us about your routine.

Danny: OK. Well, I get up at about half past seven. I wash at quarter to eight and then I have breakfast with the family.

Int: When do you start work?

Danny: I start work at nine.

Int: What do you do in the morning?

Danny: I talk to my secretary and then I read my emails and faxes.

Int: Do you meet people?

Danny: Yes, I meet the holiday reps at about half past ten. We have coffee at eleven o'clock in the office and talk about the guests. Then I check the hotel rooms and the swimming pool.

Int: Do you eat in the hotel?

Danny: Yes, I do. In the hotel restaurant.

Int: What do you do after lunch?

Danny: I go to the bank. Then I meet the hotel clients.

Int: Do you work in the office?

Danny: Yes, I write emails and letters and I meet the accountant at five o'clock.

Int: When do you go home?

Danny: I leave work at half past six.

Int: What do you do in the evening?

Danny: Well, I have dinner with my wife and children and at ten o'clock I watch the news on TV.

Grammar | Present Simple (questions and short answers with I/you/we)

3 Match the questions and answers.

1 Are you single?
2 What do you do in the evening?
3 When do you go to work?
4 Do you work in a school?
5 Where do you work?
6 What do you do?

a In an office.
b At half past eight.
c I have dinner with my husband.
d I'm a computer programmer.
e No, I'm not.
f No, I don't.

4 Rewrite the sentences as questions. Then write a short affirmative (✓) or negative (✗) answer.

You get up at nine o'clock. (✓)
Do you get up at nine o'clock? Yes, I do.
We have a DVD player. (✗)
Do we have a DVD player? No, we don't.

1 You live in New York. (✗)

_____

2 We have a French dictionary. (✗)

_____

3 You work in an office. (✗)

_____

4 You like package holidays. (✓)

_____

5 We have her phone number. (✓)

_____

5 Write questions for the answers.

Where do you live?
I live in Sydney, Australia.

1 *Where do yo wrok .*
I work in a hospital.

2 *are you a doctor*
No, I'm not a doctor. I'm a nurse.

3 *what time goes to we*
I go to work at half past eight.

4 *Do you have luhch in hos*
No, I don't have lunch in the hospital.

5 *When do you go to work*
I leave work at half past six.

6 *what do you in your*
I go to a nightclub with my friends in the evening.

Vocabulary | holidays

6 Make questions and answers using the prompts and the clocks.

you go bed? / I
When do you go to bed?
I go to bed at half past eleven.

1 you get up? / We

_____
_____

2 we have lunch? / We

_____
_____

3 you leave the office? / I

_____
_____

4 we have dinner? / We

_____
_____

Vocabulary | verbs

1 **a** Find ten more verbs in the word square and write them below. (→↓↘)

W	F	I	N	I	S	H	R
O	R	W	A	T	C	H	J
R	L	E	A	V	E	M	Q
K	G	O	A	S	V	A	W
M	E	E	T	D	H	K	F
B	T	S	L	F	E	E	D

finish

1	_____	6	_____
2	_____	7	_____
3	_____	8	_____
4	_____	9	_____
5	_____	10	_____

b Use verbs from Ex. 1a and the words in the box to label the pictures.

> the children ~~hair~~ to bed a newspaper
> dinner home

wash hair

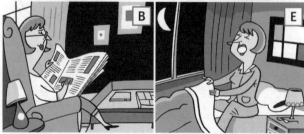

Grammar | Present Simple: *he/she/it*

2 **a** Complete the text with verbs from Ex. 1a.

Melanie has an interesting job – she's a hairdresser for film stars and she *works* in a film studio. In the morning Melanie (1) _____ up at seven o'clock. She (2) _____ the children then has breakfast. She (3) _____ home at half past eight and she (4) _____ to the film studio at nine. Melanie (5) _____ interesting people in her job. All day she (6) _____ and dries the film stars' hair. Sometimes in the afternoon she (7) _____ the actors or the films in the studio. She (8) _____ work at six o'clock and she goes home. She (9) _____ dinner and in the evening she (10) _____ the newspaper or listens to music – no films for her! She (11) _____ to bed at half past eleven.

b Read the text and look at the pictures in Ex. 1b. Write the correct order of the pictures.

a ☐ b ☐ c ☐ 1 d ☐ e ☐ f ☐

Reading

3 Read about Julian's day and write sentences in the table.

I'm a shop assistant in a big electrical shop. My day starts at half past six – I <u>get up</u> and <u>wash</u>. Then I have breakfast at quarter past seven and I <u>leave</u> home at quarter to eight. The shop opens at half past eight and I start work. I <u>work</u> in the home electrical part of the shop and I <u>sell</u> TVs, videos and DVDs. I <u>like</u> my job – it's interesting and I <u>talk</u> to a lot of people. I have lunch at half past twelve, then my work finishes at half past four. I usually <u>play</u> football with friends for about an hour. I have dinner at six o'clock and I <u>watch</u> TV in the evening. I <u>go</u> to bed at eleven o'clock.

JULIAN'S DAY	
6.30	*Julian gets up and washes.*
7.15	
7.45	
8.30	
12.30	
4.30	
6.00	
11.00	

Pronunciation

4 Complete the table with the correct form of the <u>underlined</u> verbs in the text.

/s/ STARTS	/z/ OPENS	/ɪz/ FINISHES
gets	*leaves*	_____
_____	_____	_____
_____	_____	_____
_____	_____	

Grammar | Present Simple: questions (he/she/it)

5 **a** Put the words in the correct order to make questions.

day does Julian's start What time ?
What time does Julian's day start?

he 7.00 get up Does at ?
Does he get up at 7.00?

1 Where Julian does work ?
_____

2 the shop What time open does ?
_____

3 sell Does cameras he ?
_____

4 Does his job he like ?
_____

5 after he does work do What ?
_____

6 he do What at does 6.00 ?
_____

7 CDs in the evening Does listen to he ?
_____

8 What time bed he does go to ?
_____

b Answer the questions in Ex. 5a.
Julian's day starts at half past six.
No, he doesn't. He gets up at half past six.

1 _____
2 _____
3 _____
4 _____
5 _____
6 _____
7 _____
8 _____

Writing

6 Sharon is a secretary and a student. Use the information in the table below to write about Sharon's day.

MORNING – SECRETARY IN A LAWYER'S OFFICE	
7.30	get up, have breakfast
8.30	walk to work
9.00	open the office
9.30–1.00	organise the lawyer's day, make phone calls
AFTERNOON – SPANISH STUDENT	
2.00	go to Spanish class
5.00	leave school
6.30	have dinner
8.00–11.00	do homework, watch TV
11.15	go to bed

In the morning, Sharon is a secretary in a lawyer's office. She gets up at half past seven and has ...

_____
_____
_____
_____
_____
_____
_____
_____
_____
_____
_____
_____

Vocabulary | everyday objects; adjectives; colours (VB p84)

1 **a** Find and circle the words in each word chain.

1

b a green ewspaperediaryellowalletelevision

2

usefulampicturescissorshoexcitingoldishorrible

3

taxinterestingreyoungoodiscarefulaptop

b Write the words from the word chains in the table.

OBJECTS	COLOUR ADJECTIVES	OTHER ADJECTIVES
bag	green	useful

c What do these sentences describe? Find words from the 'objects' column.

It's a kind of computer. _laptop_

1 It's black and white, and we read it.

_____

2 We look at these in museums. _____

3 We play it on a DVD player or a computer – it has music or films on it. _____

4 This is yellow in New York. _____

5 We watch films and other things on it.

_____

6 We have this on the desk, to help us read.

_____

7 You write meetings in it. _____

Grammar | *this, that, these, those*

2 **a** Match the bags to the questions.

1 What's this? ☐
2 What's that? ☐
3 What are these? ☐
4 What are those? ☐

b Use the pictures to answer the questions.

1 What's this? It's a …

_____

2 What's that?

_____

3 What are these? They're …

_____

4 What are those?

_____

3 **a** Read the dialogue. Write the questions from Ex. 2b in gaps 1–4.

Woman: Hello. You have some nice things.
(1) _____? On the table?

Man: It's a printer. It's very good.

Woman: Oh, I think my niece wants a printer.
And (2) _____?

Man: They're discs, computer discs.

Woman: Very useful ... and
(3) _____?

Man: Oh, they're dishes.

Woman: Dishes?

Man: Yes, breakfast dishes.

Woman: But they're pink!

Man: Is that a problem?

Woman: No, no ... (4) _____?

Man: It's a picture.

Woman: I know it's a picture, but what's the green thing?

Man: That's my old car. It's beautiful!

Woman: Mmm.

b **2.2** Listen and check your answers.

Pronunciation

4 **a** Look at the dialogue again. Find words with the same sound.

this (/ɪ/): _things_, _it_, _____, _____,
_____, _____, _____,
_____

these (/iː/): _____, _____

b Listen again and check your answers.

Grammar | noun plurals

5 **a** What are the plural forms of the words in the table? Use a dictionary to check.

	SINGULAR	PLURAL
1	address	_____
2	car	_____
3	diary	_____
4	family	_____
5	foot	_____
6	half	_____
7	mouse	_____
8	wife	_____
9	scarf	_____
10	sheep	_____
11	suitcase	_____
12	tomato	_____

b Complete the sentences. Make the nouns plural and change the verb if necessary.

I always take one suitcase on holiday.
We always _take_ two _suitcases_ on holiday.

1 She has a problem with her foot.
They _____ problems with their _____.

2 He wants to wash the car.
They _____ to wash the _____.

3 I like my red and green scarf.
We _____ our red and green _____.

4 The holiday home is for one family.
The holiday homes _____ for two _____.

5 Write your address on the form.
Write your _____ on the forms.

6 I use a desk diary all the time.
We _____ desk _____ all the time.

7 He always eats a tomato for breakfast.
They always _____ _____ for breakfast.

Grammar | Present Simple: negative

1 Look at the information in the table. Use it to complete the text with the positive or negative form of *to like* or *to go*.

	like				go			
	restaurants	bars	nightclubs	sports centres	to concerts	shopping	for walks	to the gym
ANDY	✓	✓	✗	✗	✓	✓	✗	✗
ROS	✗	✓	✓	✓	✓	✗	✓	✓

It's interesting that very different people sometimes meet and become friends … or husband and wife. Andy and Ros are married, but they are very, very different.

Andy is a journalist and he works a lot. In the evening he likes to relax. He doesn't want to be active. He *likes* restaurants and bars but he *doesn't like* nightclubs or sports centres. He doesn't dance or do sports. At the weekend he (1)_____ to concerts and he (2)_____ shopping, but he (3)_____ for walks or to the gym.

Ros works in an office. Her job is very boring and she likes to do exciting things in the evening and at weekends. In the evening she (4)_____ to go to bars and nightclubs, or to the sports centre, but she (5)_____ restaurants. At the weekend, she (6)_____ for walks and to the gym. Sometimes she (7)_____ to a concert with Andy, but she (8)_____ shopping at all.

2 Complete the text with the negative form of a suitable verb from the box.

> ~~like~~   listen to   relax   speak   want to   watch

Evenings at home with all the family are horrible! I like music, the radio and the TV but my daughter Sally *doesn't like* the radio – she thinks it's boring. My mother (1) _____ TV and my children don't like that! My sister Helen (2) _____ music. My husband and my father (3) _____ talk to people in the evening, and my son Justin (4) _____ to his sister because she doesn't like his friends. So, it's difficult for me in the evenings because I (5) _____!

3 Read the text and correct the sentences below.

I do lots of things at the weekend.

I often meet my friends at the shops on Saturday morning and we go shopping, then we have lunch in a café.

Sometimes I have a game of tennis in the park on Saturday afternoon or I swim and sunbathe at the swimming pool.

In the evening I go to the cinema.

On Sunday I like to relax,

and I usually stay at home.

Isabel has lunch at home on Saturdays.

Isabel doesn't have lunch at home on Saturdays.
She has lunch in a café.

1 She plays tennis at the sports centre.

She doesnt plays tennis

2 She meets her friends at the gym.

She ...s

3 She watches films at home in the evening.

She ent watchi

4 She swims at the beach.

She dosent swim
She swims i swim po

5 She relaxes at a club on Sundays.

_Sh ..._

Vocabulary | days of the week

4 **a** Complete the puzzle with five days of the week. Which day isn't in the puzzle? Write it below.

```
              M
              O
  S A T U R D A Y
              A
            D Y
  D       D A
  A       A Y
  Y     D Y
          A
          Y
```

Day not in the puzzle: _____

b Write the correct days of the week on the pages from the calendar.

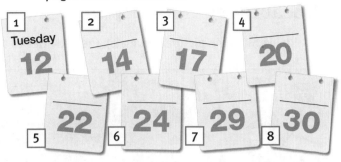

| 1 Tuesday 12 | 2 14 | 3 17 | 4 20 |
| 5 22 | 6 24 | 7 29 | 8 30 |

Reading and writing

5 **a** Read the text and complete the diary for Ivan.

My name's Ivan. I live in the south of France. I'm very active. My week is very busy. On Mondays, I swim in the sea or in the swimming pool. On Tuesdays, I go to the gym and then I go to a dance class. On Wednesdays, I ride my bike in the mountains but on Thursdays, I stay at home and relax. On Fridays, I play tennis or football with friends. At the weekend, I usually go skiing.

Monday 4	Thursday 7 _stay at home_
swim in sea / swimming pool	
Tuesday 5 _go to dance_	Friday 8 _play tennis_
Wednesday 6 _ride on hill_	Saturday 9 / Sunday 10

b Now look at Alana's diary and write a short text about her. Use *and*, *but* or *or* if possible.

Monday 4	Thursday 7
watch TV/a video	go for a walk
Tuesday 5	Friday 8
listen to music and read a book	play computer games with Jan
Wednesday 6	Saturday 9 / Sunday 10
meet friends in a café	relax at home sunbathe on the beach

My name's Alana. I live in the south of France. I'm
very relaxed. On Mondays, I _____

_____

_____

_____

_____

Vocabulary | sports and games (VB p85)

1 **a** Look at the picture and match the activities to the nouns below.

1	judo	A	6	dancing	H
2	swimming	B	7	football	J
3	riding a bike	C	8	sailing	D
4	skateboarding	D	9	running	F
5	yoga	G	10	tennis	E

b Write the verbs for the activities, using *go*, *play* or *do* if necessary.

A *go sailing*   E _____   I _____
B _____   F _____   J _____
C _____   G _____
D _____   H _____

2 **a** <u>Underline</u> the odd one out.

do: aerobics judo <u>sailing</u>

1 go: swimming riding my bike running
2 play: dance computer games tennis
3 do: football yoga aerobics
4 go: skiing running computer games
5 play: football tennis yoga

b Correct the mistakes with the verbs.

I ~~do sailing~~ every weekend. *go sailing*

1 We go riding our bikes to work. _____
2 Do you play aerobics? _____
3 We swimming at the swimming pool.
   _____
4 My brother does computer games every
   evening. _____
5 They go judo twice a week. _____

Reading

3 **a** Read the text and choose the correct title.

People say that members of a family often have the same abilities. Look at people in different jobs and you can see that it's true. Here are some examples:

■ In sport, we have the famous footballer brothers Gary and Phil Neville, and in tennis Marat Safin and his sister Dinara, and Richard Krajicek and his half-sister Michaela.

■ In show business everyone knows Julia Roberts. Not a lot of people know her brother Eric, but he also acts. Michael Jackson and his sister Janet are both famous singers, and the brothers Joel and Ethan Coen are both famous for the interesting films they make together.

■ But it isn't only brothers and sisters – Kinsley Amis and his son Martin are both famous British writers, and of course, George Bush and his father, also George, are both politicians in the USA.

1 Famous brothers and sisters ☐
2 Famous fathers and sons ☐
3 Famous families ☐

b Match the people to the activities.

1	Richard and Michaela Krajicek	a	act.
2	Julia and Eric Roberts	b	sing.
3	The Neville brothers	c	play tennis.
4	Kingsley and Martin Amis	d	play football.
5	The Coen brothers	e	write books.
6	Marat and Dinara Safin	f	play tennis.
7	Michael and Janet Jackson	g	make good films.

Grammar | *can/can't*

4 Write sentences about the people in the text, using *can*.

1 *Richard and Michaela Krajicek can both play tennis.*

2 _____

3 _____

4 _____

5 _____

6 _____

7 _____

5 a Complete the dialogue with *can* or *can't*.

A: Good morning, Miss Randall. Let me ask you a few questions. We have about sixty children here all the time. *Can* you organise games for sixty children?

B: Yes, I (1) _can_. I do that in my job now.

A: Oh, good. And how about your skills? Can you sing?

B: Yes, I (2) _can_ sing and dance. I can't paint but I (3) _can_ draw.

A: OK. Now, sports. We want our organisers to help the children learn sports.

B: Well, I can ride a bike and I (4) _can_ play tennis.

A: Good. Can you teach any other activities, for example, judo?

B: No, not judo, but I (5) _can_ teach aerobics.

A: Can you play the guitar?

B: No, I (6) _can't_.

A: Now, we have ch[...]
Can you speak o[...]

B: Yes, I (7) _can_ [...]
Spanish.

A: French?

B: No, I (8) _can_ [...]

A: OK. And can you [...]

B: Yes, I (9) _can_ [...]

A: Thank you, Miss R[...]. That's all for now. Please wait in the restaurant.

b Which activities can and can't Miss Randall do? Make a list.

She can sing and dance.

She can draw but she can't paint.

She created bike and can play

she can draw.

Pronunciation

6 a 3.1 Listen to the dialogue and check your answers.

b Listen again for the pronunciation of *can* and *can't*. Tick (✓) the correct column.

	/ə/	/æ/	/ɑː/
Can you organise games ...?	✓		
Yes, I can.		✓	
1 I can sing.			
2 ... but I can draw.			
3 I can play tennis.			
4 ... I can teach aerobics.			
5 No, I can't.			
6 I can speak German ...			
7 I can't speak French.			
8 Yes, I can.			

1 a `3.2` Cover the tapescript and listen to three phone calls. Number them in the correct order 1–3.

- ☐ a message on an answering machine
- ☐ a phone call to an office
- ☐ a voicemail message

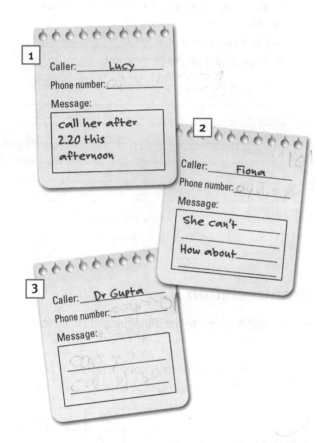

1

Caller: _____Lucy_____

Phone number: _____

Message:

call her after 2.20 this afternoon

2

Caller: _____Fiona_____

Phone number: _____

Message:

She can't _____

How about _____

3

Caller: ___Dr Gupta___

Phone number: _____

Message:

_____

_____

b Listen again and complete the messages.

2 a Complete the gaps in this dialogue.

A: Hello. Davis and Davis.

B: Good afternoon. Can I (1) _____ to Michael Jenkins?

A: I'm afraid he's not here today. Can I (2) _____ a message?

B: Yes. Can you (3) _____ him to phone Dr Gupta?

A: Of course. (4) _____ your number?

B: It's 894 7701.

A: Dr Gupta, 894 7701. Anything else?

B: Yes, (5) _____ you ask him to call after half past four?

A: Of course.

B: Thanks. Bye.

A: Goodbye.

b Check your answers with the tapescript.

EXERCISES 1 AND 2 TAPESCRIPT

1

A: Thank you for calling your Tel-call voicemail service. You have one message.

B: Hi Daniel, it's Lucy. Can you call me this afternoon after twenty past two? My number's 09404 8832. Thanks.

2

A: This is Phil and Isabel's phone. We're not here at the moment so please leave a message with your name and number after the tone.

B: Phil? It's Fiona. I can't see you tomorrow because there's an important meeting at my office. How about ten past seven on Friday? You can call me on 0991344562.

3

A: Hello. Davis and Davis.

B: Good afternoon. Can I speak to Michael Jenkins?

A: I'm afraid he's not here today. Can I take a message?

B: Yes. Can you ask him to phone Dr Gupta?

A: Of course. What's your number?

B: It's 894 7701.

A: Dr Gupta, 894 7701. Anything else?

B: Yes, can you ask him to call after half past four?

A: Of course.

B: Thanks. Bye.

A: Goodbye.

3 Find five more mistakes in this phone conversation and write the corrections.

A: Hello.

B: Hello. Can I speak ~~of~~ *to* Clare Higgins?

A: I'm afraid she isn't there today. Can I make a message?

B: Yes. Can you speak her to call Erik Langley at the bank?

A: Of course. What are your number?

B: I am 02099543301.

A: OK. Goodbye.

B: Bye.

Vocabulary | large numbers

4 **a** Match the numbers in the box to the gaps in the sentences.

An epic drama of adventure and exploration

2001: a space odyssey

8,760   1,285,000,000   175,000,000
20,000,000   20,000   2001

The population of Australia is *20,000,000*.

1 My favourite film is Kubrick's _____ *A Space Odyssey*.

2 _____ people live in Brazil.

3 Our favourite book is _____ *Leagues under the Sea* by Jules Verne.

4 A year has _____ hours.

5 _____ people live in China.

b Write the numbers in words.

twenty million

1 _____
2 _____
3 _____
4 _____
5 _____

Pronunciation

5 **a** **3.3** Listen and <u>underline</u> the strong sounds.

1 fourteen   3 fifteen   5 eighty
2 forty   4 fifty   6 eighteen

b **3.4** Listen and tick (✓) the sentences you hear.

1 a) I'm fifteen years old. ☐
   b) I'm fifty years old. ☐

2 a) That's $18.90. ☑
   b) That's $80.19. ☐

3 a) Our address is 70 Grove Road. ☑
   b) Our address is 17 Grove Road. ☐

4 a) It costs €14.40. ☐
   b) It costs €40.14. ☐

5 a) We have sixty DVDs. ☐
   b) We have sixteen DVDs. ☐

How to ... | making suggestions and requests

6 Make requests from the prompts. Use *ask, come, meet* or *take*.

to the office / tomorrow
Can you come to the office tomorrow?

1 Anna / to call me / after 6.30
   _____
   _____

2 me / at the hospital / at 7.15
   _____
   _____

3 Simon / to phone Mum and Dad / at the weekend
   _____
   _____

4 to the shop / on Tuesday / after 5.00
   _____
   _____

5 the children / to school / tomorrow
   _____
   _____

7 **a** Complete gaps a–f with the words in the box.

---
don't   can   How   ~~we~~   Let's   about   Why

☐ Dorian: No, I'm at work at 6.30. Why don't *we* meet at eight o'clock?

☐ Annabel: OK. How (a) _____ Luigi's Italian restaurant in Green Street?

☐ Annabel: (b) _____ about dinner at the Chinese restaurant?

1️⃣ Dorian: What (c) _____ we do tonight?

☐ Dorian: No, I don't like Chinese food. Why (d) do_____ we go to an Italian restaurant?

☐ Annabel: OK. (e) _____ go to the Pizzeria in Nelson Street. Can you meet me at 6.30?

☐ Annabel: OK. Eight o'clock at the pizzeria.

☐ Dorian: No, I don't like Luigi's. (f) Why_____ don't we go to a pizzeria?

b Number the sentences in the correct order (1–8).

Grammar

Verb *to be*, questions, negatives and short answers

1 **a** Complete the gaps with *am, is, isn't, are* or *aren't*.

1 Where __is__ she from?
2 How old _____ you?
3 What _____ it?
4 Who _____ he?
5 _____ you married?
6 _____ she a student?
7 _____ he Russian?
8 __are__ they from Colombia?
9 Where _____ São Paulo?
10 What _____ they?

a No, he _____.
b No, I _____ not.
c It _____ a mobile phone.
d Yes, she _____.
e He _____ Bill Clinton.
f No, they _____.
g They _____ mobile phones.
h It _____ in Brazil.
i I _____ nineteen.
j She _____ from Poland.

b Now match the questions (1–10) and answers (a–j).

Possessive *'s* and possessive adjectives

2 Choose the correct word in italics.

1 Is Hillary Clinton Bill Clinton's sister? No, she's *her/his* wife.
2 Excuse me. Are you Maria's cousin? No, I'm *her/his* husband.
3 Is David *your/you* son?
4 Is Elizabeth *their/their's* grandmother?
5 Clara is *Antonio/Antonio's* girlfriend.
6 I'm from England and *me/my* wife is from Scotland.
7 Gregory is a lawyer but *his/their* two sons are artists.
8 We are Canadian but *my/our* parents are from Turkey.
9 Prince Harry is Prince *Williams/William's* brother.
10 My sister and I live with *we/our* grandfather.

Present Simple

3 Complete the sentences with the correct form of the verb in brackets.

Julia __watches__ television in the evening. (watch)
Stephen __doesn't like__ classical music. (not like)

1 My sister _____ in a restaurant. (work)
2 David _____ the bus to work. (not take)
3 We _____ at half past seven. (get up)
4 I _____ dinner at eight o'clock. (have)
5 John _____ lunch in his office. (have)
6 Mrs Dawson _____ to work by car. (go)
7 Susan _____ her car on Saturday morning. (wash)
8 The children _____ to school at the weekend. (not go)
9 My mother _____ in the city. (not live)
10 I _____ traffic jams. (not like)

4 Make questions from the prompts.

she / live / in London?
Does she live in London?
Where / he / eat lunch?
Where does he eat lunch?

1 William / leave home / at eight o'clock?
_____

2 When / you / start work?
_____

3 Where / your parents / go on holiday?
_____

4 you / work / in an office?
_____

5 she / have / a fax machine?
_____

6 What time / he / get home?
_____

7 When / Emily / feed her children?
_____

8 you / like / nightclubs?
_____

9 they / go / to the beach at the weekend?
_____

10 Where / you / work?
_____

this, that, these, those

5 Look at the picture and complete the dialogue with *this*, *that*, *these* or *those*.

A: Do you like _____ lamps?

B: No, I like _____ lamp.

A: Do you like _____ chair?

B: No, I like _____ chairs.

Noun plurals

6 Write the plural form of the noun in the correct column. (There are two nouns in each column.)

	add -s	add -es	remove -f, add -ves	remove -y, add -ies	irregular
address		addresses			
book	books				
1 child					
2 city					
3 diary					
4 knife					
5 person					
6 picture					
7 scarf					
8 watch					

can/can't

7 Write questions and answers from the prompts.

you/play tennis? (Yes)

Q *Can you play tennis?*

A *Yes, I can.*

Darius/speak French? (No)

Q *Can Darius speak French?*

A *No, he can't.*

1 you/sing? (Yes)

Q Do you sing

A Yes me thindsing

2 your husband/cook? (No)

Q Did your husband

A No he didnt

3 she/speak Spanish and Portuguese? (Yes)

Q What languages that

A speak

4 you/do judo? (Yes)

Q _____

A _____

5 a DVD-player/send emails? (No)

Q _____

A _____

Vocabulary

8 **a** Tick (✓) the correct box.

	jobs	family	possessions	verbs	days
1 accountant	✓				
2 daughters		✓			
3 do					
4 finish			✓		
5 get up				✓	
6 nurse	✓				
7 play			✓		
8 Sunday					✓
9 uncle	✓	✓			
10 wallet					✓

b Put the words from Ex. 8a in the correct sentence.

1 Caroline works in a hospital, she is a _____.

2 I'm an _____; I work in an office.

3 My father's brother is my _____.

4 We have two _____: Jane and Mary.

5 I have €50 in my _____.

6 What time do you _____ in the morning?

7 We _____ work at six o'clock.

8 I _____ yoga at the gym.

9 We _____ tennis on Wednesday afternoon.

10 Do you go to work on Saturday and _____?

9 Match the activities (1–10) with the places (a–j).

1	see a film	a	gym
2	dance	b	concert hall
3	go for a walk	c	cinema
4	buy things	d	beach
5	sunbathe	e	restaurant
6	have dinner	f	school
7	listen to music	g	home
8	do aerobics	h	park
9	watch TV	i	shop
10	learn English	j	nightclub

Vocabulary | food and drink (VB p85)

1 a Complete the food and drink words with letters from the box.

> am as an ea ee ee el il is in ~~pp~~ tt ff ol gg

a**pp**les

1 b____f
2 br___d
3 bu____er
4 ch___se
5 co____ee
6 c___a
7 cr____ps
8 l___b
9 m___k
10 or___ge juice
11 p____ta
12 p____eapples
13 e___s
14 waterm____ons

b Write the words from Ex. 1a in the table below. One word can go in two places!

	MEAT	FRUIT	DRINKS	DAIRY	OTHER
Countable		apples			
Uncountable					

2 Find these things in the picture and write the words.

convenience food *hot dog*

1 tropical fruit _____
2 fish _____
3 vegetable _____
4 meat _____

Grammar | countable and uncountable nouns

3 Correct the mistakes.

I drink a lot of ~~milks~~ every day.
milk

1 Tea are popular in England.
   _____

2 We have a cereal for breakfast.
   _____

3 I buy a kilo of rices every week.
   _____

4 Do you eat a lot of meats?
   _____

5 People say sugar are bad for you.
   _____

6 Can I have 250 grammes of butters, please?
   _____

7 I like a French bread.
   _____

8 Do you like tunas?
   _____

9 I think mineral water are very nice.
   _____

Grammar | *How much?/How many?*

4 Write questions with *How much* or *How many*.
Then write answers that are true for you.

apples / you / eat / every week
How many apples do you eat every week?
I eat three apples every week.

1 rice / you / buy / at the supermarket
_____?
_____

2 water / you / drink / every day
_____?
_____

3 oranges / you / buy / at the market
_____?
_____

4 bananas / your family / eat / every week
_____?
_____

5 coffee / you / drink / at the weekend
_____?
_____

Vocabulary | quantities and prices

5 Write the quantities in words.

950g   *nine hundred and fifty grammes*

1 25kg _____
2 630g _____
3 719g _____
4 4.5l _____

6 a Match the prices to the words.

1 €7.75   a seven hundred and seventy-five euros
2 €75.75   b seven euros and fifty-seven cents
3 €77.05   c seven hundred and fifty-seven euros
4 €775   d seventy-five euros and seventy-five cents
5 €77.50   e seventy-seven euros and five cents
6 €757   f seventy-five euros and fifty cents
7 €7.57   g seventy-seven euros and fifty cents
8 €75.50   h seven euros and seventy-five cents

b How do we say these prices? Tick (✓) three correct phrases and cross (✗) the incorrect one.

1 €3.75
  a) three euros and seven five ☐
  b) three euros seventy-five ☐
  c) three euros and seventy-five cents ☑
  d) three seventy-five ☐

2 $8.95
  a) eight dollars and ninety-five cents ☑
  b) eight ninety-five ☐
  c) eight dollars and nine five cents ☐
  d) eight dollars ninety-five cents ☐

How to ... | say quantities and numbers

7 This is Julia's weekly shopping list. Complete the questions and answers.

6 apples
2kg rice
1.5kg cereal
3l milk
250g coffee
3 bananas
12 eggs
4 oranges

How much milk does Julia buy?
She buys 3 litres.

1 _____?
  She buys 250 grammes.
2 _____?
  She buys four.
3 _____ does Julia buy?
  _____ two kilos.
4 _____ eggs _____?
  _____
5 _____ cereal _____?
6 _____?
  _____ three.
7 _____?
  _____ six.

Vocabulary | containers

1   **a** Rewrite the letters to make five containers.

N A C   *can*

1   T O T L E B _____
2   O X B _box_
3   C O R A N T _carton_
4   T E K C A P _packet_
5   G A B _bag_

b Label the pictures with words from Ex. 1a.

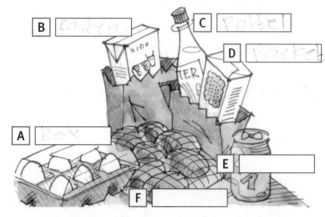

c Complete the phrases with a container word.

1   a _packet_ of crisps/potatoes
2   a _bottle_ of water/olive oil
3   a _____ of eggs/chocolates
4   a _can_ of cola/tuna
5   a _carton_ of fruit juice/milk
6   a _____ of biscuits/cereal

Grammar | *a/an*, *some* and *any*

2   Write the list of ingredients. Use *a/an* or *some* and the words in the box.

> butter cheese papaya pasta tuna salad
> tomato ~~pineapple~~ water

1   _a pineapple_
2   _a papaya_
3   _____
4   _____
5   _water_
6   _____
7   _butter_
8   _____
9   _____

Chicken and pineapple pasta

3   Complete the dialogue with *a/an, some* or *any* and the word in brackets, in the plural if necessary.

A: Let's write our shopping list for the supermarket.

B: OK. I think we want *some mineral water* (mineral water).

A: No, we don't need (1) _____ (mineral water). We have six bottles. We don't have (2) _____ (fruit juice).

B: OK. Now, get *some eggs* (egg) and (3) _____ (cheese) – we can have an omelette tonight.

A: Right. Do we have (4) _____ (potato)?

B: Yes, we do. Oh, get (5) _____ (chocolate) for my mother too – a nice big box, please. Do you have (6) _____ (money)?

A: Well, I don't have (7) _____ (cash) but I have (8) _____ (credit card).

B: OK. Do you want a cup of coffee before you go?

A: Yes, please! And can I have (9) _____ (biscuit) too – just one?

B: No, we don't have (10) _____ (biscuit). Put biscuits on the shopping list!

Pronunciation

4   **a** Underline the syllables with /æ/ (p**a**sta) and /ʌ/ (s**o**me) in these words. Then put the words in the correct column.

> business**man** carrot grandparents hungry
> laptop money nightclub package
> programme sunbathe Sunday unemployed

A /æ/ *pasta*	B /ʌ/ *some*
businessman	

b **4.1** Listen and check your answers.

Vocabulary | adjectives

5 Match the adjectives to the descriptions.

1 hungry — a You feel this when everything in your life is good.

2 happy — b You feel this when everything in your life is bad.

3 healthy — c You feel this when you want to sleep.

4 fit — d You feel this when you want to eat.

5 tired — e You feel this when you want to drink.

6 thirsty — f You are this when you eat and drink the right things.

7 unhappy — g You are this when you eat and drink the wrong things.

8 unhealthy — h You are this when your body is in good condition.

Reading and writing

6 Read the text. Write short answers to questions 1–8 on the right.

1 Who is Laurence's letter to?
Amanda

2 Who is the letter about?
Jane

3 How old is Jane?
_17_

4 What does she do in the evenings?
goes to nightclubs

5 How does she feel in the mornings?
tired

6 What are the problems with her diet?
She has burgers and pizza

7 What does Jane think of school?
she hates school

8 Does she do her homework?
no she doesn't

7 Amanda's letter to the magazine tells Laurence about her daughter and asks for his help. Follow the steps to write her letter.

1 Complete the main part of the letter, about Jane's problems. (Use your answers to Ex. 6, questions 2–8.)

2 Now write the start and end of the letter.

Dear Amanda

I'm sorry to hear about your daughter, Jane. It's very bad that she goes to nightclubs all the time and doesn't come home until one in the morning, at the age of only 17. I can understand that she's tired every morning and doesn't want to go to school! Young people need a lot of sleep and your daughter doesn't have much sleep. Also, a lot of convenience food like burgers and pizza is not very healthy for a girl of her age. I think Jane is probably very unhappy. You need to talk to her and ask her some questions, for example, why does she hate school and why doesn't she do any homework? Why don't you take Jane out one evening to a nice restaurant and talk to her? She probably wants to talk to you but doesn't know how to start.

Good luck.
Laurence

I have a problem with my daughter, Jane. She's only ___17___ but she hates ___school___.
Also, she goes out ___to nightclubs___.

Her diet is also very bad. I give her healthy food at home but she ___eats burgers and pizza___.

What can I do? Please help me.
take her out to a nice restaurant

Super Pizza

Free delivery!

PIZZAS	small	large
cheese and tomato	€5.95	€6.95
tuna, cheese and tomato	€6.75	€7.75
beef and mushroom	€8.25	€9.25
tuna and pineapple	€7.50	(1)_____
chicken and mushroom	€7.95	(2)_____

SIDE ORDERS		
fries	€2.25	€3.35
tomato salad	(3)_____	€3.00
tuna salad	v3.00	€3.99

DRINKS		
mineral water	€1.25	€2.15
coffee	(4)_____	(5)_____
cola	€1.95	€2.35
orange juice	€3.25	€3.95

Call 09909700700 to order.

We accept all major credit cards or you can pay cash on delivery.

EXERCISE 1 TAPESCRIPT

Super Pizza: Hello, Super Pizza.

Marisa: Hi. How much is a large chicken and mushroom pizza?

Super Pizza: That's eight euros ninety-five.

Marisa: And how much is a small tomato salad?

Super Pizza: Two euros forty-five.

Marisa: What about coffee?

Super Pizza: A small cup of coffee is two euros and a large coffee is two euros seventy-five.

Marisa: OK. Do you have a tuna and pineapple pizza?

Super Pizza: Yes.

Marisa: How much is a large one?

Super Pizza: Eight euros fifty.

Marisa: Fine. I'd like a large tuna and pineapple pizza.

Super Pizza: Any side orders?

Marisa: Yes. Can I have a small tomato salad?

Super Pizza: Sure. What about a drink?

Marisa: A small coffee, please.

Super Pizza: Right. A large tuna and pineapple pizza, a small tomato salad and a small cup of coffee.

Marisa: How much is that?

Super Pizza: That's twelve euros ninety-five.

Marisa: Can I pay by credit card?

Super Pizza: Of course. What's the name on the card?

Marisa: It's Marisa Sánchez …

Listening

1 **a** 4.2 Cover the tapescript and listen to the phone call. Answer the questions.

1 Does Marisa order a pizza?

2 Does she order a drink?

3 How does Marisa pay for the food?

b Listen again. What exactly does Marisa order? Complete the notes.

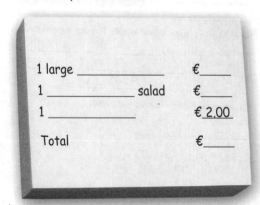

1 large _____ €_____

1 _____ salad €_____

1 _____ € 2.00

Total €_____

c Listen again and complete the prices on the menu.

2 **a** Write the questions for these answers. Use the information in the menu.

How much is a small cheese and tomato pizza?

It's €5.95.

1 _____

It's €8.50.

2 _____

It's €3.00.

3 _____

It's €8.25.

b Match the questions and answers. Use the information in the menu.

1 Do you have pizzas?

2 Can I pay by credit card?

3 How much is a large coffee?

4 Do you have burgers?

5 Anything to drink?

6 Any side orders?

a Yes, I'd like a mineral water.

b No, we don't.

c Yes, you can.

d It's €2.75.

e Yes, large fries, please.

f Yes, we do.

Grammar | object pronouns

3 a You are Janine. This is the lunch order for your office. Read the notes and complete the picture labels with object pronouns.

Today's lunch order
Janine: burger and fries
Janine, Steve and Lucy: 3 cups of coffee
Peter: a cheeseburger
Alicia: a tuna sandwich and a bottle of mineral water
Linda and Erik: 2 small pizzas

for *me*

1 for _____   3 for _____

2 for _____   4 for _____

b You are Janine. Replace the word(s) in brackets with an object pronoun and complete the answers.

Are the two small pizzas for (Lucy) *her*?
No, *they are for them.*

1 Are the fries for (Linda and Erik) _____?
No, _____.

2 Are the three cups of coffee for (Peter) _____?
No, _____.

3 Is the sandwich for (Janine, Steve and Lucy) _____?
No, _____.

4 Is the cheeseburger for (Alicia) _____?
No, _____.

5 Is the bottle of mineral water for (Linda and Erik) _____?
No, _____.

4 Replace the underlined expressions with pronouns and rewrite the sentences.

Our grandmother and grandfather live with me and my brothers.
They live with us.

1 Danny loves Isabel.
_____

2 My boyfriend and I don't like meat.
_____

3 Our teachers help me and my classmates with our homework.
_____

4 My parents visit my grandparents every Saturday afternoon.
_____

5 My brothers and I play football with John.
_____

6 Mrs Field uses her computer every day.
_____

7 Do you and your friends want to have lunch with me and my friends?
_____

How to ... | order food in a fast food restaurant

5 Choose the correct words or phrases in italics.

A: Hello, what can I get you today?
B: I'd (1) *want / like* a tuna, cheese and tomato pizza, please.
A: Small or large?
B: How (2) *much / many* is the large pizza?
A: It's €7.75.
B: OK, large, please.
A: Right. A large tuna, cheese and tomato pizza. Any side orders?
B: (3) *Are / Do* you have fries?
A: No, we don't. Do you (4) *want / like* a salad?
B: OK. A small tomato salad.
A: Anything to (5) *eat / drink*?
B: Yes, (6) *I'm / I'd* like a large cup of coffee, please.
A: OK.
B: How much (7) *are / is* that?
A: That's €10.95.
B: Can I pay (8) *by / of* credit card?

Pronunciation

6 a 4.3 Listen to this list. The arrow ↗ shows when the voice goes up, and ↘ shows when the voice goes down.

A large tuna and pineapple pizza [↗], a small tomato salad [↗] and a small cup of coffee [↘].

b 4.4 Listen to these lists and write ↗ in the spaces if the voice goes up, and ↘ if the voice goes down.

1 I'd like a large cheeseburger ☐, a small cup of coffee ☐ and a small salad ☐.
2 I'd like a small vegetarian pizza ☐, large fries ☐ and an orange juice ☐.
3 I'd like a kilo of oranges ☐, an apple ☐, two bananas ☐ and a melon ☐.
4 I'd like 500g of beef ☐, a packet of biscuits ☐, 200g of sugar ☐ and a bottle of mineral water ☐.

Reading

Las Palomas Village

Thank you for asking for information about Las Palomas Village.

Las Palomas is in the south of Spain, a short drive from Málaga. Las Palomas is the perfect place for holidays, or for a home by the sea, especially for retired people. Only twenty-eight kilometres from Málaga Airport, Las Palomas is perfect for long weekends, but it isn't just a holiday village – it's also a home.

At Las Palomas there's a small supermarket and there's a bank. There are three bars and two restaurants serving international food. There are two large swimming pools and there's a well-equipped gym. You can also walk to the local beach in just five minutes, where you can find a variety of shops and beach restaurants. There isn't a cinema or a hospital in the village, but Málaga is only a short bus ride away.

There are forty-two apartments at Las Palomas, with one, two or three bedrooms, and there are four luxury villas. You can buy your apartment with furniture, if you want. The furniture includes all modern kitchen equipment, beds, sofas, cupboards and dining tables and chairs. Each apartment has a private terrace. Prices start from 200,000 euros.

You can visit Las Palomas any time. Please call the number above to organise your visit.

1 a Look at the text. What kind of text is it?

1 an advert in a magazine ☐

2 information in answer to a letter ☐

b Read the text. What is there at Las Palomas? Tick (✓) the correct pictures.

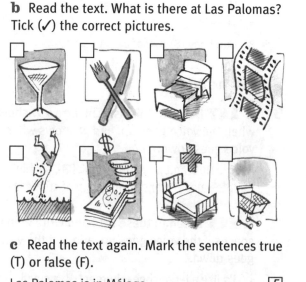

c Read the text again. Mark the sentences true (T) or false (F).

Las Palomas is in Málaga. `F`

1 There aren't any shops at Las Palomas. ☐

2 You can change money in the village. ☐

3 You can swim in the sea near the village. ☐

4 There are a lot of shops near the village. ☐

5 There aren't any cinemas in the village. ☐

6 You can't buy an apartment with furniture. ☐

7 Each apartment has a private garden. ☐

Vocabulary | equipment and furniture

2 a Write the correct vowels (a, e, i, o, u) in these furniture and home equipment words.

1 B O T H
2 B E D
3 CD PL A Y A R
4 CH A I R
5 C oo K E R
6 C U P B oa R D
7 D E S K
8 D I SH W A SH E R
9 DVD PL A Y E R
10 FR I D G E
11 M I C R O W A V E
12 S O F A
13 SH O W E R
14 T A B L E
15 T E L E V I S I O N
16 T oi L E T

b Put the words from Ex. 2a into the word map.

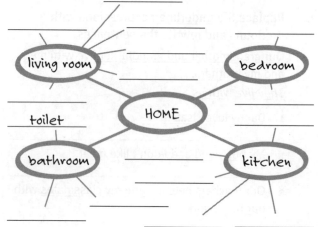

Grammar | *there is/there are*

3 Complete the sentences with the correct form of *there is/are*. Use the contracted forms. (Some need questions or negatives.)

There's a famous zoo in Berlin.

1 _____ sixteen classrooms in our school.
2 _____ any shops near here?
3 _____ a good Chinese takeaway in the centre of the town.
4 _____ any meat in this meal, so you can eat it.
5 _____ a gym on the ship?
6 _____ a garden with the apartment but there is a large terrace.
7 _____ any eggs in the fridge. Can you get some?
8 _____ a message for you on the answering machine.
9 _____ a concert in the concert hall this Saturday?

4 a Look at the plan of the holiday village and correct the mistakes in the sentences on the right.

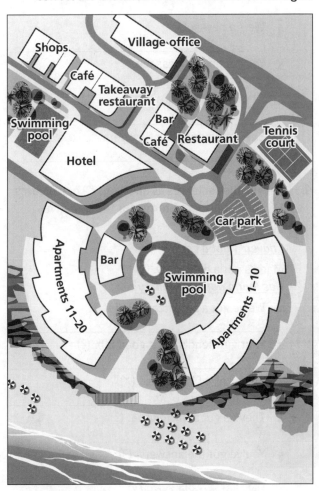

There are thirty apartments in the village.
There are twenty apartments.

1 There's one swimming pool.
_____

2 There isn't a beach near the village.
_____

3 There aren't any cafés in the village.
_____

4 There isn't a place to park your car.
_____

5 You can't play tennis here.
_____

b Write sentences about the village with *there is/are* (or *there isn't/aren't*).

(nightclubs) *There aren't any nightclubs in the village.*

1 (a hotel) _____
_____

2 (bars) _____
_____

3 (a takeaway restaurant) _____
_____

4 (shops) _____
_____

5 (a tennis court) _____
_____

6 (a school) _____
_____

7 (banks) _____
_____

Lifelong learning | Personalise it!

5 Write sentences about your home, using the words in brackets.

(CD player) *I have a CD player in my bedroom.*
(bathroom) *There are two bathrooms in my apartment.*

1 (television) I have a television in my bedroom
2 (bed) I have bed in my bed room
3 (cupboard) there isn't cupboard in my bedroom
4 (dishwasher) there is dishwasher in my kitchen
5 (dining room) there isn't dining room in my house

Vocabulary | possessions (VB p84)

1 **a** Match letters in A with letters in B to make the names of furniture, equipment and personal possessions (some are two words).

A	B
1 answering	a player
2 arm	b board
3 book	c machine
4 CD	d shelves
5 micro	e washer
6 cup	f wave
7 dish	g table
8 dining	h chair

1 *answering machine* _____
2 *armchair* _____
3 _____
4 _____
5 _____
6 _____
7 _____
8 _____

b Use five words from Ex. 1a to label the pictures.

1 _____
2 _____
3 _____
4 _____
5 _____

2 What is it? Match the words and phrases in the box to the sentences in the next column.

> bed fridge ~~cooker~~ car laptop computer
> sofa washing machine MP3 player
> television dining chair

You can cook meals on it. *cooker*

1 You can use it to listen to music. _____
2 You can drive it. _____
3 Two or three people can sit on it. _____
4 You can watch it. _____
5 You can sleep in it. _____
6 You can put milk in it. _____
7 You send emails from it. _____
8 Only one person can sit on it. _____
9 You can wash clothes in it. _____

Grammar | have got

3 Write sentences with *have/has got*. Use contracted forms.

Jenny / an apartment in the city
Jenny's got an apartment in the city.

1 I / two brothers
_____

2 They / a swimming pool
_____

3 Álvaro / an MP3 player
_____

4 We / a new sofa
_____

5 You / a phone message
_____

6 I / three children
_____

7 She / a boyfriend in New York
_____

4 Rewrite the sentences as questions (?) or negatives (✗). Use contracted forms for the negatives.

I've got a car. (✗)
I haven't got a car.

Maria's got a dictionary. (?)
Has Maria got a dictionary?

1 We've got a big kitchen. (✗)
_____

2 Your girlfriend's got a good job. (?)
_____

3 She's got a DVD player. (✗)
_____

4 They've got a microwave. (?)
_____

5 You've got the answers. (?)
_____

6 He's got a credit card. (✗)
_____

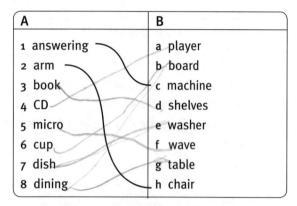

5 Make questions from the prompts and write true short answers.

your town / theatre?

Has your town got a theatre?

Yes, it has.

1 your town / shopping centre ?

_____

_____

2 your town / airport ?

_____

_____

3 you / any children ?

_____

_____

4 you / any brothers or sisters ?

_____

_____

6 Write three sentences with *have got* and *but,* like the examples. Write about you and your family. Use the personal possessions in Ex. 1 and 2.

I've got a cooker but I haven't got a microwave. My sister's got a washing machine but she hasn't got a car.

1 _____

_____

2 _____

_____

3 _____

_____

Listening ✶

7 **a** `5.1` Cover the tapescript. Listen to Serena. Where does she live? Tick (✓) the correct picture.

b Listen again and complete the sentences with *have/has got* and a number.

Their house *has got four* bedrooms.

1 Serena and Harry _____ children.

2 Serena _____ cats.

3 Harry _____ computers.

4 They _____ DVDs.

c Listen again and answer the questions. Use short answers.

Has Serena got an apartment in the city?

No, she hasn't.

1 Have Serena and Harry got any children?

_____

2 Has Serena got a car?

_____

3 Has her husband got a car?

_____

4 Has Serena's house got a terrace?

_____

5 Have they got a dining room?

_____

6 Have they got a widescreen TV?

_____

EXERCISE 7 TAPESCRIPT

I live in a big house in the country with my husband, Harry. The house has got four bedrooms and a big garden. We've got two children and three cats – they love the garden. They play in it every day. And we've got a garage – I haven't got a car but my husband has. I'm an artist and I work at home. I use one of the bedrooms. It's got a big terrace. I can sit on the terrace in the summer and paint the garden – it's lovely. Harry's a computer programmer. He's got three computers. Actually, he's got lots of electronic things in the house. He's got a digital camera and he makes DVDs. In fact we've got forty DVDs now. In the evenings we eat dinner in the kitchen – we haven't got a dining room. Then we watch TV in the living room – we've got a fantastic widescreen TV.

Pronunciation

8 `5.2` Listen to the underlined sounds in these words and tick (✓) the correct box.

	/ɒ/	/æ/
g<u>o</u>t	✓	
c<u>a</u>t		✓
1 h<u>o</u>spital	☐	☐
2 p<u>o</u>cket	☐	☐
3 t<u>a</u>p	☐	☐
4 sh<u>o</u>p	☐	☐
5 p<u>a</u>cket	☐	☐
6 h<u>o</u>t	☐	☐

Vocabulary | landscapes and adjectives to describe places (VB p85)

1 **a** Complete the crossword with adjectives and places, using the clues. Then answer the question below.

			¹C			D			
		²L							
³B					⁴F				
				⁵G					
⁶H				⁷I				⁸D	
					⁹B			Y	

Clues

New York is a [6 across] [1 down] – millions of people live there.

There's a [8 down] [2 down] in my country – there isn't any water in it.

The New Forest is a [3 across] [4 down] in the south of England.

Kefallonia is a very [5 across] [7 across] – it has a lot of trees.

Copacabana in Rio de Janeiro is a very [9 across] [3 down] – a lot of people go there.

One adjective from the crossword isn't in the clues. Which adjective? _____

b Cross out the adjective that we don't use to describe the place.

river: dangerous ~~modern~~ wide

1 desert: hot dry green
2 mountain: friendly high cold
3 city: dry noisy busy
4 beach: popular huge modern
5 island: green wide tropical
6 forest: old busy beautiful
7 lake: green dry small

Grammar | modifiers

2 Write a sentence with your opinion about these things. Use a modifier and the adjective given.

Football / exciting *Football is really exciting. / Football isn't very exciting.*

1 Nightclubs / exciting _____

_____

2 Our classroom / comfortable _____

_____

3 Television / relaxing _____

_____

4 My diet / healthy _____

_____

5 Computer games / interesting _____

_____

3 **a** Look at the pictures. Choose one modifier and one adjective to describe each picture, and write them under the picture.

Modifiers: quite ~~very~~ very really not very not very
Adjectives: big famous healthy high popular ~~wide~~

very wide river

_____

_____

_____

_____

_____

b Now write a sentence to describe each picture, using the prompts.

The Amazon / river *The Amazon is a very wide river.*

1 Traffic warden / job

_____

2 The Empire State / building

_____

3 The Volkswagen Polo / car

_____

4 Brad Pitt / actor

_____

5 Chicken and potatoes / meal

_____

Writing

4 **a** Read the text about John and his city. There aren't any capital letters or full stops. Correct the text, following the example. (See Writing bank on page 145 of your Students' Book.)

> J   S   B   .
> john is from scotland, in the north of britain ⋀
>
> he lives in edinburgh, a large city in the south-
>
> east of the country
>
> there are lots of interesting places in
>
> edinburgh: museums, cinemas, theatres and
>
> restaurants there's an arts festival every year
>
> and john always goes to it with his friends
>
> the city is also quite near beautiful lakes and
>
> mountains
>
> john likes edinburgh because it's a very friendly
>
> place he also thinks the city is very beautiful,
>
> but he doesn't like the scottish weather – it's
>
> very cold!

b Find phrases in the text that express these ideas. Underline the phrases and write them in the table.

HOW TO ...	
say where someone lives	*John is from ...*
describe a country/city	
give someone's opinion	

5 Write an email to a friend about your town/city. Follow these steps.

1 Look at the email on page 51 of your Students' Book. How do you start the email?

2 Say where you live.

3 Write two or three sentences to describe your town/city.

4 Give your opinion about your town/city.

5 End the email.

> Thanks for your email. Here's the information about my town. I live in _____
>
> _____
>
> _____
>
> _____
>
> _____
>
> _____
>
> _____
>
> _____
>
> _____
>
> _____

Pronunciation

6 **a** Mark the syllables in these words and underline the strong syllable.

1 a/<u>part</u>/ment 2 <u>bar</u>/gain 3 comfortable
4 compare 5 decide 6 famous 7 mountain
8 opinion 9 tropical 10 village

b [5.3] Listen and check your answers.

c Write the words in the table. Listen again if you want.

WORDS WITH TWO SYLLABLES		WORDS WITH THREE SYLLABLES	
Stress on 1st syllable	Stress on 2nd syllable	Stress on 1st syllable	Stress on 2nd syllable
bargain			*apartment*

Vocabulary | buildings (VB p85)

1 Use the clues to complete the crossword.

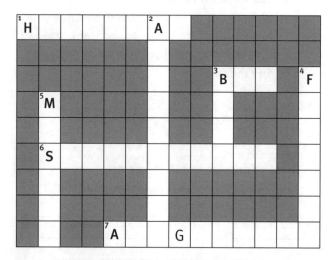

1 Doctors and nurses work here.
2 You can live here.
3 [across] You can drink (and sometimes eat) here.
3 [down] You can put your money here.
4 People work here – they make things.
5 You can look at old things here.
6 You can buy all your food and drinks here.
7 You can look at pictures here.

Grammar | past of *to be*

2 Look at the maps. Write sentences about Summertown in 1990.

There are offices in Green Street.
There were cottages in Green Street.

1 There's a theme park in Lake Road.

_____

2 There's a supermarket in Lake Road.

_____

3 There are apartments in Station Road.

_____

4 There's a museum in Station Road.

_____

5 There's a nightclub in Harley Street.

_____

6 There's a hotel in Harley Street.

_____

7 There's a sports centre in the park.

_____

3 Write questions about Summertown. Then answer them.

there / supermarket / Lake Road / 1990?
Was there a supermarket in Lake Road in 1990?
No, there wasn't. There were shops.
What / there / the park / 1990?
What was there in the park in 1990? There were houses in the park.

1 there / factory / Station Road / 1990?

_____

_____

2 What / there / Green Street / 1990?

_____

_____

3 there / nightclub / Harley Street / 1990?

_____

_____

4 there / apartments / Station Road / 1990?

_____

_____

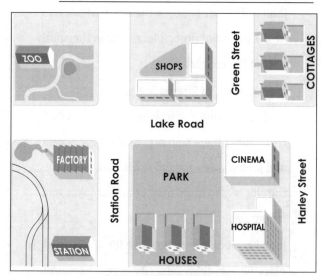

Summertown 1990

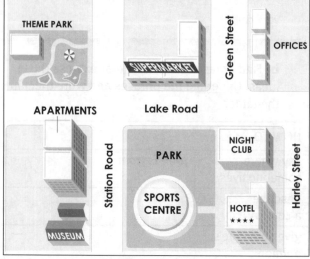

Summertown now

Grammar | Past Simple of regular verbs: positive

4 Angie is a famous singer. Look at her diary for last week and complete the sentences.

Monday	10	17	clean the house!
Tuesday	11	18	play football with boys (afternoon)
Wednesday	12 visit new concert hall 3.00p.m.	19	TODAY
Thursday	13	20	
Friday	14 perform at concert hall 8.30p.m.	21	
Saturday	15 open new supermarket 10.30a.m.	22	
Sunday	16 watch video of concert with Mike, 4.00p.m.	23	

Angie visited the new concert hall last Wednesday.

1 She _____
   _____ last Friday evening.

2 _____
   _____ last Saturday morning.

3 _____
   _____ on Sunday afternoon.

4 _____
   _____ two days ago.

5 _____
   _____ yesterday.

5 **a** Complete the text with verbs from the box in the Past Simple.

> cook help play relax ~~start~~ walk
> watch work

Luisa's Day

Luisa's day _started_ at 8.00a.m. yesterday. She
(1) _____ to work at 9.00 and she
(2) _____ from 9.30 to 4.30. Then she
(3) _____ tennis with a friend from 4.30
to 5.30. At home she (4) _____ dinner
for her family then she (5) _____ her
son with his school work. In the evening she
(6) _____ a video and she
(7) _____ .

b Now write about Warren's Day.

> start – 6.30a.m.
> walk to bus stop – 7.00
> wait for bus – 7.15 to 7.30
> work – 8.00 to 4.00
> repair cars all day
> cook dinner
> study – 7.30 to 9.30
> listen to music

Warren's Day

Warren's day started at 6.30a.m. yesterday. He _____
_____
_____
_____
_____
_____
_____
_____

Reading

6 **a** The dialogue below is not in the correct order. Write the correct numbers in the boxes.

☐ I <u>decided</u> to have a sandwich in the office, so I stayed at work at lunchtime.

☐ But you weren't at home at eight o'clock in the evening.

[1] Where were you yesterday? I wanted to talk to you. I phoned you at 8.30 in the morning.

☐ Yes, I was. I cooked dinner for the children, then I listened to CDs all evening.

☐ Oh, I walked to work yesterday, so I wasn't at home at 8.30.

[9] Oh, well, never mind. Can I ask you something now?

☐ Well, I visited my friend Rosie in hospital after work, at about six o'clock, for an hour.

☐ But I called you again at lunchtime and you weren't at home.

☐ What about after work? I phoned you again at half past five.

b 🔊 **6.1** Listen and check your answers.

Pronunciation

7 **a** <u>Underline</u> the regular Past Simple verbs in Ex. 6a and write them in the table.

/t/ WORKED	/d/ OPENED	/ɪd/ DECIDED

b Listen again and check your answers.

6.2

Vocabulary | prepositions of place

1 Look at the picture and read the sentences. Write the names of the food and drink next to the letters below.

The salad is in the sink. The apples are on the table and the potatoes are under the chair. The meat is in the microwave. The pasta is behind the microwave and the eggs are in the fridge. The biscuits are between the microwave and the sink. The milk is in the fridge and the orange juice is next to it. The bread is next to the TV.

A _milk_   B _eggs_ C ____   D ____   E ____
F ____   G ____   H ____   I ____   J ____

2 Work out where the people in the study group sit, and write the names on the correct desks.

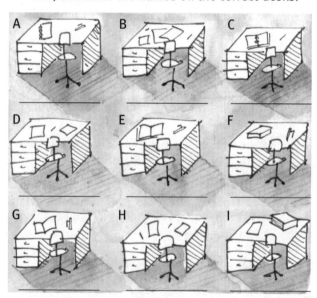

Steve sits in front of Stephanie and next to Susan.
Sally sits in front of Sandy and next to Susan.
Simon sits behind Susan and in front of Sean.
Simon sits on the right of Stephanie.
Sean sits between Sam and Sarah and behind Simon.
Sam sits on the left of Sean.

Grammar | Past Simple: questions

3 a Write questions in the Past Simple, using the prompts.

1 you / have / a good holiday?
Did you have a good holiday?

2 Where / you / go? _Where did you go?_

3 you / stay / in a nice place?
_____

4 What / you / do?
_____

5 you / meet / any friends?
_____

6 How long / you / stay?
_____

7 When / you / get home?
_____

8 you / buy me / anything?
_____

b Match the questions in Ex. 3a to these answers.

☐ Yes, we did. We stayed in a really good hotel.
☐ Yesterday evening.
☐ To Munich, in the south of Germany.
☐ Yes, we did. We know some people there.
☐ No, I didn't. I'm sorry.
☐ We visited lots of museums and galleries.
☐ 1 Yes, we did. It was great, thanks.
☐ We stayed for a week.

Lifelong learning | Words and pictures

4 Draw arrows or stars (as in the examples) to remind you of the directions and positions.

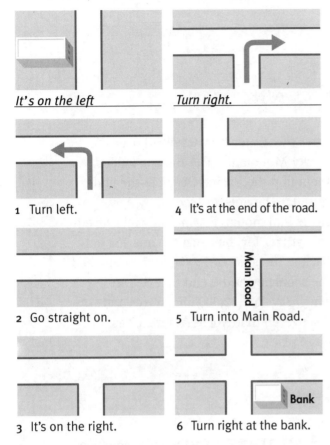

It's on the left

Turn right.

1 Turn left.

4 It's at the end of the road.

2 Go straight on.

5 Turn into Main Road.

3 It's on the right.

6 Turn right at the bank.

Listening

5 a **6.2** Listen to four dialogues and follow the directions on the map. You are at the station. Write the letters of the places.

1 the art gallery ☐

2 the church ☐

3 the hospital ☐

4 the swimming pool ☐

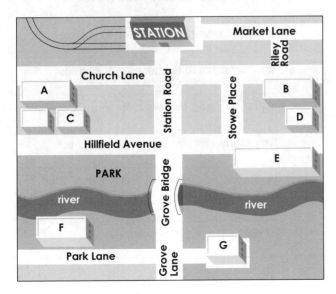

b Use the map to help you complete the dialogues. Then listen again and check your answers.

1 A: Excuse me, can you *tell me the way* to the art gallery?

B: Of course. Go out of the station and _____ _____ into Church Lane. Then turn right into Stowe Place and left _____ _____ _____ _____ the road. The art gallery is on the _____.

2 A: Excuse me, do _____ _____ the way to the church?

B: Yes, it's easy. Leave the station and turn _____ _____ Church Lane. The church is at the end of the road, _____ _____ _____ _____.

3 A: Excuse me, is there a hospital near here?

B: A hospital? Yes. Go out of the station and go straight _____. Go across the bridge at the end of Station Road and _____ _____ into Park Lane. The hospital is _____ _____ _____.

4 A: Excuse me, can you _____ _____ _____ _____ to the swimming pool?

B: Yes. Leave the station and go _____ on. Go along Station Road and go _____ the river into Grove Lane. Then _____ _____ into the park. The swimming pool is in front of you.

Writing

6 Write directions from the station. The cinema is building B, the supermarket is C and the bank is building D.

1 Excuse me, can you tell me the way to the cinema?
Yes, of course. Go out of the station and _____ _____ _____

2 Excuse me, do you know the way to a supermarket?
Yes, there's a supermarket in Hillfield Avenue. You go straight _____ _____

3 Excuse me, is there a bank near here?
Yes, there is. Go out of the station and turn left into _____ _____

Reading

1 **a** Read the text quickly, and answer the question.

How long was Lewis and Clark's journey? _____ years

LEWIS AND CLARK

Meriwether Lewis and William Clark are famous American explorers. In 1804 President Thomas Jefferson wanted a map of the western United States because at that time people didn't know the area west of the Mississippi River. Lewis and Clark started from St Louis in 1804 with thirty men and an Indian woman, Sacagawea. The weather was very bad and it was difficult to travel. They stayed for the winter with the Dakota Indians.

After the winter they travelled over the Rocky Mountains. The Indians helped them find the Pacific Ocean at the end of 1805. They discovered many new rivers and mountains and they measured everything for their maps. They started back at the start of 1806 and they finished their journey at the end of the year. They travelled 12,900 kilometres and discovered that North America was a huge place.

b Read the text again and number the events 1–7, in the order they happened. (Use a dictionary to check any new words.)

They stayed with the Dakota Indians. ☐

They finished their journey to the Pacific Ocean. ☐

The President wanted a map of the western US. ☐ 1

They started back after the winter. ☐

They travelled over the Rocky Mountains. ☐

Lewis and Clark started from St Louis. ☐

The weather was very bad. ☐

c Now answer these questions.

Why did the President want a map of the western United States?

Because people didn't know the area west of the Mississippi River.

1 How many people were there on the journey?

_____

2 Who helped them find the Pacific Ocean?

_____

3 What did they measure?

_____

4 What did they discover?

_____

Grammar | Past Simple: negative

2 Use the prompts to write negative sentences in the Past Simple.

Christopher Columbus / invent / the compass

Christopher Columbus didn't invent the compass.

Charles Darwin / be / American

Charles Darwin wasn't American.

1 William Shakespeare / write / *Don Quixote*

_____

2 My great-grandparents / own / a car

_____

3 Queen Elizabeth I / be / married

_____

4 We / have / mobile phones in the 1970s

_____

5 My father / go / to university

_____

6 He / study / foreign languages at school

_____

7 In ancient times people / eat / a lot of food and they / be / tall _____

_____

8 I / do / my homework yesterday

_____

Vocabulary | transport (VB p85)

3 Complete the puzzle with forms of transport.

```
        T □ □ □
    C   R □ □ □
      T A □
      B I □ □ □ □
  P □ A N □ □
      B S
```

4 Make true sentences.

	The Peugeot 305		an invention	ship
1	The *Titanic* and the *Lusitania*	is	popular	in New York
2	The TGV and the Talgo	are	Columbus's	ships
3	Yellow taxis	was	famous	car
4	The railway	were	fast	trains
5	The *Santa Maria*		a French	of the nineteenth century

The Peugeot 305 is a French car.

1 _____

2 _____

3 _____

4 _____

5 _____

Pronunciation

5 **a** <u>Underline</u> the stressed words in the answers.

1 A: Did you see a film?
 B: No, we saw a <u>concert</u>.

2 A: Do you like pasta?
 B: No, I like potatoes.

3 A: Are you French?
 B: No, I'm Canadian.

4 A: Is the child hungry?
 B: No, she's thirsty.

5 A: Did you arrive on Friday?
 B: No, we arrived on Thursday.

b `6.3` Listen and check your answers.

Writing

6 **a** Think about a great journey from your past. Make notes to answer these questions.

1 Where did you go?

_____

2 Who was with you on the journey?

_____

3 When was it?

_____

4 When did it start and finish?

_____

5 What did you visit?

_____

6 How did you travel?

_____

7 Where did you stay?

_____

8 How long was the journey?

_____

9 What did you like?

_____

10 What didn't you like?

_____

11 Why was it 'a great journey'?

_____

b Write your notes into a narrative of about 100 words. Write your narrative in your notebook.

c Read your narrative and check it for grammar, spelling and punctuation, then rewrite it.

Grammar

Countable and uncountable nouns

1 Put these nouns into the correct column in the chart below.

> armchair biscuit bread coin dishwasher
> mayonnaise money receipt rice salad

COUNTABLE NOUNS	UNCOUNTABLE NOUNS

How much?/How many?; a/an, some and any

2 Choose the correct word in italics.

1 I'd like *some/any* cheese, please.
2 How *much/many* meat do you eat every week?
3 Is there *some/any* milk in the fridge?
4 Simon always takes *a/some* cream in his coffee.
5 How *much/many* students are there in the class?
6 I can't see you now. I haven't got *some/any* time.
7 Have you got *any/a* DVD player?
8 How *much/many* bathrooms are there?
9 Please give me *some/a* carton of orange juice.
10 Can you go to the shop, please? Here's *some/any* money.

Object pronouns

3 Complete the sentences with an object pronoun.

1 That's my coffee. It's for _____.
2 It's John's dictionary. Please give it to _____.
3 'Is that Maria and Olaf on the bus?' 'Yes, it's _____.'
4 That's Eddie's new car. Do you like _____?
5 Your girlfriend's on the phone. She wants to speak to _____.
6 'That's Sophie's sister in the photo.' 'Yes, I know _____.'
7 That's my credit card. Please give it to _____.
8 Tony likes our house. He always stays with _____ when he comes to London.
9 'Have some fries with your burger.' 'No, thanks. I don't like _____.'
10 'Is that Sarah in the shop?' 'Yes, that's _____.'

there is/there are

4 Complete the dialogue with a form of *there is/there are*.

A: I think I'd like to take the apartment, but what furniture (1) _____ in the living room?
B: Well, (2) _____ a big sofa.
A: (3) _____ a dining table?
B: Yes, (4) _____, and (5) _____ four dining chairs.
A: Oh, good. (6) _____ a coffee table?
B: No, (7) _____.
A: OK. (8) _____ any bookshelves?
B: No, (9) _____.
A: Oh, and what about a television, or a music system?
B: No, (10) _____ any electrical equipment.

Modifiers

5 Choose the correct modifier and write sentences.

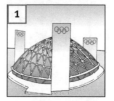

quite / really unhappy my sister today
My sister is really unhappy today.

1 very / not very the new sports centre modern
_____
2 really / quite this film boring
_____
3 not very / really late we
_____
4 really / quite my diet unhealthy
_____
5 very / not very well-equipped the kitchen
_____

have got

6 Write questions using the prompts. Then answer them with short answers. (✓) = Yes, (✗) = No.

Alex / an MP3 player (✗)
Has Alex got an MP3 player? No, he hasn't.

1 you / a microwave? (✗)

_____
_____

2 Sarah / a credit card? (✓)

_____
_____

3 your parents / a big garden? (✗)

_____
_____

4 we / any biscuits? (✗)

_____
_____

5 the dog / any food? (✓)

_____
_____

Past Simple

7 **a** Write the Past Simple forms of these verbs.

1 be   _____   6 stop   _____
2 decide _____   7 travel _____
3 marry   _____   8 visit   _____
4 open   _____   9 want   _____
5 start   _____   10 work   _____

b Complete the text with Past Simple verbs from Ex. 7a. Use the negative if you see *(not)*.

My father was only 16 when he (1) _____ going to school. He was unhappy at school and he (2) _____ *(not)* to study at university – he wanted to go to work. He (3) _____ in a factory for five years but he still wasn't very happy, so he (4) _____ to leave the factory and see some of the world. He (5) _____ to India and he stayed there for ten years. He (6) _____ my mother but they decided to come back to Britain to start a family. At that time, it was very unusual to have an Indian wife and people (7) _____ *(not)* very friendly to them at first. My parents (8) _____ an Indian restaurant in Bradford, in the north of England, and a lot of people (9) _____ it and enjoyed the food. After a few years, my parents (10) _____ to produce Indian food in cans for supermarkets, and this was very popular. So I was very happy when I was a child – with loving parents and lots of money!

c Correct the sentences about the text.

The writer's father stopped school when he was 14.
He didn't stop school when he was 14.
He stopped school when he was 16.

1 He studied at university.

_____
_____

2 He stayed at the factory for ten years.

_____
_____

3 He married a woman in Africa.

_____
_____

4 The writer's parents opened an Indian factory.

_____
_____

5 They produced Indian food for schools.

_____
_____

Vocabulary

8 **a** Write the words in the correct column.

> banana bathroom bed bicycle boat cola
> cupboard desk dining room hall kitchen
> lamb library motorbike newsagent's
> pharmacy post office potato table tram

FOOD & DRINK	ROOMS	FURNITURE	PLACES IN A TOWN	TRANSPORT

b Complete with words from the table.

1 We prepare food in the _____.
2 We can take a _____ between France and Britain.
3 I want to look at the new books in the _____.
4 We've got a shower in our _____.
5 I do my homework at my _____ in my bedroom.
6 I don't like a lot of meat but I like _____.
7 Can you buy a magazine for me at the _____?
8 This room is very untidy. Please put your books in the _____.

Vocabulary | adjectives for describing people (VB p84)

1 **a** Read the information and label the people in the picture.

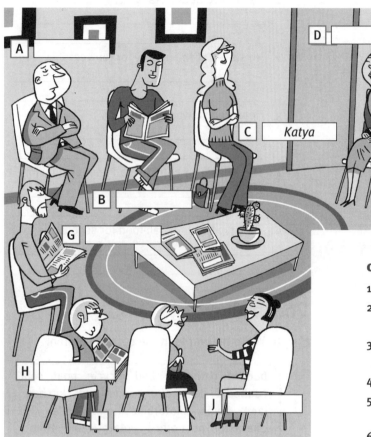

- Katya's got fair hair and she wears glasses.
- Clara's got dark hair and she's very slim.
- Amanda's middle-aged. She's got fair hair and she's quite short.
- Henry's got dark skin and a beard.
- Dieter's got fair hair and he's very tall. He's quite handsome.
- Surinda's very friendly. She's got dark skin.
- Melanie's young and pretty. She's got pale skin and fair hair.
- Jeremy's bald.
- Alvaro's handsome. He's got dark hair and he's quite tanned.
- Stefan's quite fat. He's got fair hair.

b Complete these sentences about the picture with numbers or adjectives.

Three people wear glasses.

1 Five people have got _____ hair.
2 _____ people have got a beard.
3 _____ people are middle-aged.
4 _____ people have got dark hair.
5 Two men are _____.

c Complete with words from Ex. 1a.

1 I wear _____ when I read.
2 It was very sunny last week so now I am quite _____.
3 Deirdre's very tall but her parents are quite _____.
4 Do you think Bruce Willis is _____ or ugly?
5 Chinese and Japanese people usually have _____ hair.
6 Uncle Malcolm's got a _____.
7 Young women film stars are often very _____.
8 My children are very _____ – they talk to everyone!

2 Complete the sentences with a suitable adjective. (The adjectives are not all in Ex. 1.)

1 Sam doesn't like going to parties and meeting new people. He's _____.
2 Mrs Barrett is 98. She's very _____.
3 Philip doesn't have a handsome face. He's quite _____.
4 We like our teacher very much. She's really _____.
5 Jane is lovely but I don't like her husband. He's _____.

3 Write a sentence describing each of these people.

1 A member of your family.
   _____
2 A famous film star or pop star.
   _____
3 Your best friend.
   _____

Lifelong learning | Opposite adjectives

4 Match the adjectives (1–10) with their opposites (a–j). Use a dictionary.

1	comfortable	a	tiny
2	huge	b	modern
3	quick	c	good
4	early	d	exact
5	married	e	interesting
6	bad	f	late
7	old-fashioned	g	poor
8	boring	h	uncomfortable
9	rich	i	single
10	approximate	j	slow

Grammar | pronoun *one/ones*

5 Match the words in italics in the text (1–6) to the words below.

sports centre ☐   shopping ☐ *1*   badminton ☐
shopping centre ☐   CDs ☐   salad ☐

I love shopping but my husband hates (1) *it*. There is a big shopping centre in our town and there is a small (2) *one* near our house. We go there every Saturday morning. I go to the supermarket and get the food. My husband usually goes to the bookshop and buys CDs. He likes classical (3) *ones*. Then we have lunch. I usually have a small salad and my husband has a large (4) *one*. In the afternoon we go to the sports centre. It's a modern (5) *one* with a gym and a swimming pool. My husband uses the gym. I play badminton – I love (6) *it*!

6 Rewrite the sentences using *one* or *ones*.

My girlfriend's got a car but I haven't got a car.
My girlfriend's got a car but I haven't got one.

1 I like hot places but Sally likes cold places.

_____

2 Can I have six large salads and two small salads, please? _____ .

_____

3 Do you want the British spelling or the American spelling? _____

_____

4 We've got three bedrooms – I sleep in the big bedroom. _____

_____

5 Are they the blue chairs, the red chairs or the yellow chairs? _____

_____

6 The first flat's got a terrace and the second flat's got a garden. _____

_____

7 I'd like four tuna sandwiches and a chicken sandwich, please. _____

_____

Reading and writing

7 **a** Complete the gaps (a and b) and write short answers to the questions below.

(a) _____ Jenna,

Thanks for your last letter. It was really funny! I started my International Studies course at the university last month. My first course is Spanish. I'm in the beginners' class. Our teacher is lovely. She's middle-aged and she comes from Toledo. She's very friendly. My classmates are very nice. There are three girls and five boys in the class. Two of the boys are only eighteen but the others are the same age as me – nineteen.

The lessons are quite difficult but they're very interesting. I like the grammar and the listening exercises. I do two hours of homework every day. I usually work in the university study centre because there are lots of dictionaries and some computers with really useful language programs. In the evening I go out with some of my classmates. We go to a restaurant or a nightclub – we have a lot of fun! Give my love to Mum and Dad and write again soon.

(b) _____
Florence

1 Who is the letter to? _____
2 Who is the letter from? _____
3 Are Jenna and Florence sisters or friends?

_____

4 Where does Florence study? _____
5 Where does Florence's teacher come from?

_____

6 How many students are in the Spanish class?

_____

7 Why does Florence work in the study centre?

_____

8 What does Florence want Jenna to do?

_____

b Write a letter to a close relative (brother, sister, etc.) or friend. Tell him/her about your school, your English class, your teacher and classmates. Use Florence's letter as a model.

Grammar | possessive pronouns

1 Match A–E to statements 1–5 below.

A | This flat belongs to you and your best friend.

D | Your brother's bicycle.

B | Your parents' car.

C | Your motorbike.

E | Your sister's car.

1 It's mine. ☐ 2 It's his. ☐ 3 It's hers. ☐
4 It's ours. ☐ 5 It's theirs. ☐

2 Choose the correct word in italics.

That's not your book, it's *me /mine*.

1 Can I use *your /yours* car this evening?
2 We can hear *theirs /their* television in our living room.
3 Take one of the pens, they're *ours /our*.
4 Is this dictionary *your /yours*?
5 Don't drink that coffee, it's *hers /her*.
6 We didn't finish *our /ours* dinner.
7 You can use *mine /my* umbrella.
8 Are those *her /hers* trainers?
9 The present isn't for us. It's *theirs /their*.

3 Match the underlined phrases to the expressions in the box.

is theirs   isn't ours   doesn't belong to them
~~isn't mine~~   are ours   is mine   aren't his
isn't yours   belongs to you   is ours

You can't use that computer. It <u>doesn't belong to me</u>. *isn't mine*

1 I think this book <u>is yours</u>. _____
2 That Nokia phone <u>belongs to me</u>. _____
3 The house on the left <u>belongs to Alice and her husband</u>. _____

4 The big present <u>is for us</u>. _____
5 The DVD player <u>isn't theirs</u>. It's ours. _____
6 The television <u>doesn't belong to us</u>. It belongs to my parents. _____
7 Don't drink that cup of coffee. It <u>isn't for you</u>, it's for Mauro. _____
8 Those holiday photos <u>belong to us</u>. _____
9 The chairs <u>aren't my brother's</u>. They belong to his wife. _____

4 Complete the text with the words from the box. Use each word once only.

mine his hers ours yours theirs

I live in a large apartment with my sister. It belongs to our parents. The furniture doesn't belong to me and my sister – it's all (1) _____, too. But the television and music system are (2) _____ – we bought them together last year. We've both got mobile phones: (3) _____ is a Nokia and my sister's is a Motorola. We use them a lot, but (4) _____ isn't very good because it hasn't got a camera. My phone's got a camera and it plays MP3s! My sister's boyfriend's got a really good phone. He can use (5) _____ when he travels because it works in lots of different countries. Have you got a mobile phone? Can you use (6) _____ in different countries?

Pronunciation

5 **a** **[7.1]** Listen and <u>underline</u> the sound /θ/ in these words.

1 bir<u>th</u>day
2 third
3 something

b **[7.2]** Listen and tick (✓) the words you hear.

1 a) free ☐   b) three ☐
2 a) eighth ☐   b) hates ☐
3 a) thin ☐   b) tin ☐
4 a) six ☐   b) sixth ☐
5 a) first ☐   b) thirst ☐
6 a) think ☐   b) drink ☐

Vocabulary | ordinal numbers; months

6 Answer the questions.

Which date is one month before 5th March? *5th February*

1 Which date is two months after 18th September?
   _____

2 Which month comes after May? _____

3 Which day comes between Tuesday and Thursday?
   _____

4 Which day comes after Friday? _____

5 Which date is three months before 22nd October?
   _____

6 1st July is Monday. Which day is 7th July?
   _____

7 Which date is three weeks after 3rd August?
   _____

7 Write the dates in italics in words.

America's Independence Day is on *4/7*. <u>*the fourth of July*</u>

1 *25/12* is Christmas Day.
   _____

2 William Shakespeare's birthday is *23/4*.
   _____

3 St Patrick's Day, *17/3*, is a holiday in Ireland.
   _____

4 *26/12* is a holiday in Britain, Canada and Australia.
   _____

5 Pedro Alvares Cabral discovered Brazil on *22/4*, 1500.
   _____

6 My birthday is *19/10*. _____

7 The Second World War started on *3/9*, 1939.
   _____

Listening

8 **a** **[7.3]** Cover the tapescript in Ex. 8b and listen to the conversation. Who are the food and drinks for? Complete the table with ticks (✓).

	ORANGE JUICE	CUPS OF COFFEE	CHICKEN SANDWICH	TUNA SANDWICH	BURGERS	SALAD	BAG OF CRISPS
PHIL							
ANA							
DAVE AND JOE							
SYLVIA							
DARREN							

b Complete the gaps with possessive pronouns.

Ana: Ah, Phil. You've got the food.
Phil: Yes. Here we are. Now, let's see. The chicken sandwich, that's (1) _____, Ana.
Ana: No, it isn't (2) _____. That's for Darren. He wanted chicken.
Phil: Right, sorry. The chicken sandwich is (3) _____.
Ana: Yes. And the tuna sandwich is (4) _____.
Phil: OK. Is the salad (5) _____, too?
Ana: No, that's for Sylvia.
Phil: Yes, that's (6) _____. And the cups of coffee?
Ana: They're for Dave and Joe.
Phil: Right. And the burgers are (7) _____, too, I think ...
Ana: Yes, they are. What about the orange juice and the bag of crisps? Are they (8) _____?
Phil: Yes, they're (9) _____.

c Listen again and check your answers.

Reading

1 Read the text quickly. What is it about?

  1 a new type of banknote

  2 a man who tried to steal something

  3 a problem with the police

It's a crazy world!

A man was in a Berlin police station last night after he tried to steal a 1,000 euro note from a car.

The man, a 28-year-old tourist, noticed the note inside the car in a Berlin street. The thief broke into the car and took the note, but people in the street saw him and called the police. The police arrived quickly, caught the man and put him in a police station cell.

Unfortunately for the man, the note wasn't even a real euro note – euro notes only go up to 500 euros, not 1,000. The note was in fact an advertisement for a local business. The business made the fake 1,000 euro notes to advertise a competition – people could win 1,000 euros as the top prize in the competition. The thief didn't understand that the note wasn't real!

2 Match the words 1–6 from the article to their approximate meanings a–f.

1	steal	a	false, not real
2	thief	b	sadly
3	broke into	c	went into a house/car to take something
4	cell	d	a person who takes things and doesn't ask
5	unfortunately	e	to take something from someone, and not ask
6	fake	f	a room in a police station

3 **a** Read the text again. Put the events in the correct order.

The police caught the man. ☐

A business in Berlin made some fake 1,000 euro notes. ☐1

They took him to the police station. ☐

He broke into the car and tried to steal it. ☐

People from the business put the notes in cars in Berlin. ☐

A man noticed one of the fake notes in a car. ☐

b Answer the questions with a few words only.

What did the man see?

A fake 1,000 euro note

1 Did he know it was a fake note? _____

2 What did he do? _____ _____

3 Why did the police catch him? _____

4 Was the note a real euro note? _____

5 Who made the notes? Why?

_____

_____

_____

Grammar | Past Simple: irregular verbs

4 **a** Complete the table with the Past Simple form of the verbs.

	INFINITIVE	PAST SIMPLE FORM	
		REGULAR	IRREGULAR
1	be	_____	*was / were*
2	try	*tried*	_____
3	notice	_____	_____
4	break	_____	_____
5	take	_____	_____
6	see	_____	_____
7	call	_____	_____
8	arrive	_____	_____
9	catch	_____	_____
10	put	_____	_____
11	make	_____	_____
12	can	_____	_____

b Rewrite the sentences, using the Past Simple form of verbs from the table.

Thieves often break into the nightclub.

Thieves broke into the nightclub again last night.

1 We catch the bus to work every morning.

_____

yesterday morning.

2 Don and Eva see their grandchildren once a week.

_____

last Sunday.

3 Mum makes fantastic chocolate biscuits.

_____

for the party last weekend.

4 Xavier takes hundreds of photos on every holiday.

_____

on his last holiday.

5 I can swim 500 metres in twenty minutes.

_____

when I was a child.

6 Alicia puts a lot of sugar in her coffee.

_____

in her coffee yesterday!

7 They aren't very happy about the weather.

_____

about the weather on holiday!

8 The train usually arrives on time.

_____

late yesterday morning.

Vocabulary | phrasal verbs

5 **a** There is one phrasal verb in the article in Ex. 1. What is it?

_____

b Complete the text with phrasal verbs from the box. Use the Present or Past Simple.

> get up   listen to   look after   look at
> move in   pick up

I have a nice life. I ___*get up*___ when I want in the morning and I (1) _____ the newspapers before I go to work. Then in the evening I see friends, watch TV or (2) _____ music. Last week my boyfriend asked me to (3) _____ with him for a week. His little niece, Molly, was with him and he wanted me to help. Every day I took her to school before I went to work. In the evening, I left work early and (4) _____ Molly from school, then I (5) _____ her until 7.00, when my boyfriend came home. Then I cooked and cleaned the apartment! It was awful, and I was very happy when Molly went back home at the end of the week.

Pronunciation

6 **a** **7.4** Listen. Do the question words start with the sound /w/ or /h/? Write /w/ or /h/ after each word.

1 what _____   5 why _____
2 where _____   6 how _____
3 who _____   7 whose _____
4 when _____

b Complete the questions with one of the question words. Then write answers which are true for you. Write full sentences.

1 _____ old were you on your last birthday?

_____

2 _____ did you go on your last holiday? (place)

_____

3 _____ did you do when you were there?

_____

4 _____ did you last take an exam? (time)

_____

5 _____ did you talk to yesterday evening?

_____

6 _____ did you start learning English? (reason)

_____

Vocabulary | clothes

1 Find four clothes words and one adjective in each word chain.

> 1 JACKETSHIRTIGHTOPULLOVER

clothes words: *jacket t-shirt* _____ _____
adjective: _____

> 2 DRESSHORTSHOESCARFORMAL

clothes words: _____ _____ _____ _____
adjective: _____

> 3 GLOVESMARTROUSERSUITIE

clothes words: _____ _____ _____ _____
adjective: _____

2 Write the words from the box in the correct columns. Some words can go in two columns.

> coat gloves jeans pullover scarf shorts
> suit T-shirt tie trainers

SUMMER	WINTER	FORMAL	INFORMAL

3 Label the pictures using an adjective from the box and a clothes word.

> formal loose ~~smart~~ tight thick light

Grammar | Present Simple; adverbs of frequency

4 Put the words in brackets in the correct position.

Emily ↓drives to work. (usually)

1 I wear a hat in winter. (always)
2 The weather is hot in July. (sometimes)
3 We eat at fast food restaurants. (never)
4 I use my microwave. (hardly ever)
5 My kitchen is untidy. (often)
6 She gets money from the cashpoint. (usually)
7 Formal clothes are uncomfortable. (often)

5 Put the words in the correct order to make sentences.

in the Sahara desert It rains never
It never rains in the Sahara desert.

1 wear a suit I hardly ever to work
_____

2 sometimes Mrs Gladstone late is
_____

3 my parents often We visit at the weekend
_____

4 to Greece They in the summer go usually
_____

5 my mother on Saturdays always I phone
_____

6 always The manager busy is
_____

7 gets up never early James on Sundays
_____

8 It in August hardly ever in Madrid rains
_____

| 1 | *a smart jacket* | 3 | _____ | 5 | _____ |
| 2 | _____ | 4 | _____ | 6 | _____ |

6 Rewrite the sentences using suitable adverbs of frequency. Use each adverb once only.

Dimitri goes to the gym four times a week.
Dimitri often goes to the gym.

1 Jason doesn't smoke.

_____

2 I go to the theatre once a year.

_____

3 They watch the TV news every day.

_____

4 Jennifer wears a dress once or twice a week.

_____

5 From Monday to Saturday he gets up at seven o'clock.

_____

Reading and writing

A

Dear Alison
Can you give me some (1) _____?
I work in a bank. I (2) _____ a suit and a tie and smart shoes. The bank is near my house and I usually walk to work. In the summer it is very hot and I feel very (3) _____ in my formal clothes when I walk to the bank. What (4) _____ I do?

Malcolm Grey

B

Dear Alison
(5) _____ help me? I work in a sports centre and I usually wear trainers, shorts and a T-shirt. In the morning I (6) _____ help in the gym but in the afternoon I sometimes work in the office. My colleagues in the office say I (7) _____ look smart in my shorts and T-shirt! How can I wear comfortable clothes for the gym and look (8) _____ in the office? What do you suggest?

Sophia Antrim

Answer

Comfortable casual clothes can be smart. But don't wear a T-shirt and shorts in the office! Wear (9) _____ cotton trousers and smart trainers. Wear a T-shirt but get a smart cotton top and (10) _____ it on when you go into the office. You can take it off when you work in the gym.

7 a Read the letters and the answer. Is the answer for A or B?

b Complete gaps 1–10 with words and expressions from the box.

don't wear put can uncomfortable usually smart advice light Can you

c Write the questions for these answers.
Where does Malcolm work? In a bank.

1 _____
A suit and a tie and smart shoes.

2 _____
He walks.

3 _____
In a sports centre.

4 _____
In the morning.

5 _____
She doesn't look smart.

8 Read the information and write an email to Davina in your notebook.

Next month you begin a new office job at SystemPro Incorporated, a big American computer company in your home town. You don't know very much about the company.

You want to know about these things:
• clothes
• private phone calls and emails
• smoking
• lunch breaks

Davina, one of your colleagues from your old job, now works for SystemPro Incorporated. You want her advice.

Listening

1 Look at the picture. Write the correct numbers.

He's eating a burger. ⟦3⟧   She's laughing. ☐
He's shouting. ☐   She's carrying a suitcase. ☐
He's wearing a suit. ☐   She's feeling unhappy. ☐
He's walking towards man number 6. ☐
She's smoking. ☐   He's eating a sandwich. ☐
She's waiting at the check-in desk. ☐

2   **a** [8.1] A police detective is at the airport. He is looking for Ron Tyler, a thief, and his gang. Cover the tapescript on page 53 and listen. Which number is the police officer? ☐

b Listen again and write the numbers of each of these people.

Ron Tyler ☐   Leanne Tyler, his wife ☐
Mikey Tyler, Ron's son ☐   Big Dave ☐
Tracey, Mikey's girlfriend ☐
Hayley, Ron's daughter ☐

c Listen again. Tick (✓) the eight phrases you hear.

1	I'm watching. ☐		7	She's arriving. ☐
2	He's talking. ☐		8	She's crying. ☐
3	He's calling. ☐		9	She's working. ☐
4	He's shouting. ☐		10	She's waiting. ☐
5	She's cooking. ☐		11	She's smoking. ☐
6	She's looking. ☐		12	He's walking. ☐

EXERCISE 2 TAPESCRIPT

A: Where are you, Brian?

B: I'm at the airport. I'm watching those famous thieves – the Tyler Gang.

A: Oh, good. Are they all there?

B: I think so, but I don't know all of them. I can see Ron Tyler – he's talking on his mobile phone. He's shouting. He isn't happy!

A: Is his wife there?

B: Leanne? Yes, she is. She's looking at a magazine at the bookshop. She's laughing.

A: What about Ron's son, Mikey?

B: Is he big and ugly?

A: Yes, that's Mikey!

B: I see him. He's eating a burger. Wait a minute. He's meeting someone ... yes, a young woman. She's arriving now. She's short and pretty. She's carrying a huge suitcase.

A: That's Mikey's girlfriend, Tracey. A big suitcase ... interesting. Is Ron's daughter Hayley there?

B: Yes, she's waiting at the check-in desk. She's smoking. She looks confused.

A: Hayley's always confused. What about her husband, Big Dave? He's the dangerous one ...

B: Oh, yes. Oh, no! He's watching me ... now he's walking towards me ... I'm going!

Grammar | Present Continuous

3 **a** Write about the ten numbered people in the picture. Use their names if you know them.

1 *Tracey is arriving at the airport. She's carrying a large suitcase.*

2 _____
_____

3 _____

4 _____
_____

5 _____
_____

6 _____
_____

7 _____
_____

8 _____
_____

9 _____
_____

10 _____
_____

b Make questions using the prompts. Then answer the questions.

Tracey / carry / a small bag?

Is Tracey carrying a small bag? No, she isn't.
She's carrying a large suitcase.

1 Mikey / wear / jeans?

_____

_____

2 Mikey / eat / a sandwich?

_____

_____

3 Hayley / smoke?

_____

_____

4 Big Dave / wear / a coat?

_____

_____

5 Leanne / feel / unhappy?

_____

_____

Grammar | adverbs of manner

4 **a** Complete the table with the missing adjectives or adverbs.

	ADJECTIVE	ADVERB
1	bad	_____
2	_____	carelessly
3	close	_____
4	comfortable	_____
5	_____	well
6	happy	_____
7	_____	hungrily
8	quick	_____
9	sad	_____
10	_____	strangely

b There are mistakes with the adverbs or adjectives in five of the sentences. Find the mistakes and correct them.

Are you sitting ~~comfortable~~? *comfortably*

Francisco always does his work carefully. ✓

1 Don't run so fast! _____

2 You look sadly today – what's wrong? _____

3 Marina always talks very loud. _____

4 You sing very good. Are you a singer? _____

5 Kelvin is a strangely person. _____

6 I'm really hungry. What's for dinner? _____

7 The children are playing very quiet in their room.

_____

Vocabulary | the weather

1 **a** Make seven more weather words from the boxes.

~~fog~~ wa su win sno co rain cloud

wing nny ing dy ~~gy~~ ld y rm

fog + gy = foggy

1 _____ 5 _____

2 _____ 6 _____

3 _____ 7 _____

4 _____

b Use the weather words to complete the sentences.

1 It's ___*windy*___ and _____ in the centre.

2 It's _____ and _____ in the north.

3 It's _____ and _____ in the south.

4 It's _____ in the west.

5 It's _____ in the east.

Pronunciation

2 **a** **8.2** Listen to each sentence twice. Are the underlined sounds /ɒ/ or /əʊ/? Write the number of each sound in the table.

		/ɒ/	/əʊ/
1	Joan wears new cotton tops under her old coat.	2	3
2	I lost my watch in the post office.		
3	I need some new clothes to go to college in October.		
4	It's hot in Australia but it's snowing and cold in Poland.		

b Listen again and check your answers.

Reading

3 **a** Read the text about the weather and our health. Tick (✓) the correct columns.

	GOOD FOR US	BAD FOR US	GOOD AND BAD
The sun			
Hot weather			
Cold weather			

Weather wise

Can the weather really affect our health and our moods? Read on and find out!

The sun

- The sun can be good for us. It gives us vitamin D – this is very important for young people when they are growing.
- But the sun can also be bad for us. A lot of sun can hurt our skin very badly – a good suntan really is not healthy.

Hot weather

- Hot weather can be bad for us. We lose water from our bodies and that can be dangerous. It's a good idea to drink a lot of water when it's hot.
- Very hot weather can also affect our moods. In hot weather people often get tired, have headaches and sleep badly. It can also affect people with depression quite badly.

Cold weather

- A lot of old people have problems when it's very cold because their body temperature falls quickly and they become sick.
- Some people become very depressed in cold, dark weather. They can't sleep and they don't eat a lot.
- Cold weather can be good for us too: people often feel very strong and healthy in the mountains because the cold air is very clean and relaxing.

b Read the text again. Mark the sentences true (T) or false (F).

1 It is healthy to have a nice suntan. ☐

2 Hot weather is often good for people with depression. ☐

3 The cold can affect old people very badly. ☐

4 Depressed people sometimes don't sleep very well. ☐

5 Many people think cold mountain air is depressing. ☐

Lifelong learning | Nouns and adjectives

4 Complete the table with nouns or adjectives from the text.

	NOUNS	ADJECTIVES
1	_____	healthy
2	importance	_____
3	_____	suntanned
4	_____	depressed
5	sickness	_____
6	darkness	_____

How to ... | take part in a factual conversation

5 a 〔8.3〕 Cover the tapescript. Listen to the dialogue and find:

1 a sentence giving an opinion.
_____

2 a question asking for an opinion.
_____

3 an agreement.
_____

4 a disagreement.
_____

b Look at the tapescript and check your answers.

Grammar | Present Simple and Present Continuous

6 Look at the underlined phrases in the tapescript below. Write the numbers of the phrases on the correct line.

Actions happening now: 1, _____

Actions that happen regularly: 4, _____

7 Write sentences about Jason, using the prompts in the boxes and the pictures.

Jason lives in the city and he works in a department store. Every day ...

> eat a burger with friends   play computer games
> take the bus to work   sell men's clothes

1 *He takes the bus to work.*

2 _____

3 _____

4 _____

This week Jason is on holiday. What's he doing?

> swim in the sea   play football on the beach
> eat fish at a restaurant   sunbathe on the beach

5 *He's sunbathing on the beach.*

6 _____

7 _____

8 _____

EXERCISE 5 TAPESCRIPT

Meera: Hello, Carmen. (1) <u>What are you doing</u> here?

Carmen: Hi. (2) <u>I'm waiting</u> to go on the sunbed. (3) <u>I'm trying</u> to get a good suntan before we go on holiday.

Meera: Really? Why?

Carmen: Well, I think it looks horrible if you're the only pale person on the beach. Don't you think so?

Meera: Well, no, I'm not sure. It isn't healthy to have a suntan, you know.

Carmen: Oh, I agree that you need to be careful. (4) <u>I always spend</u> just ten minutes on the sunbed. (5) <u>I never stay</u> for very long. You aren't here for the sunbed, then, Meera?

Meera: Oh, no. (6) <u>I'm meeting</u> my fitness instructor – there he is.

Carmen: Oh, (7) <u>do you often come</u> to the gym?

Meera: Yes, (8) <u>I use the gym</u> three or four times a week.

Carmen: Wow – you're very fit!

Reading

1 **a** Look quickly at the text about British newspapers.
How many newspapers does it describe? _____

British people like their newspapers.

About 70 per cent of British people read a national newspaper every day and many also read a local newspaper. There are two main types of daily newspaper in Britain. The 'broadsheets' contain national and international news, and pages on topics such as money, the arts and travel. These are the four daily broadsheets:

➔ *The Times* is very old – it started in 1785. It sells about 680,000 copies a day and it costs 50 pence.

➔ *The Guardian* started in 1821, in Manchester. (Most newspapers started in London.) It sells about 325,000 copies a day and it costs 55 pence.

➔ *The Daily Telegraph* sells more copies than the others – about 975,000 a day, and it costs 60 pence. It started in 1855.

➔ *The Independent* only began in 1986. It sells about 205,000 copies a day and it costs 60 pence.

'Tabloids' contain national news but not a lot of international news, and they have a lot of pages on sport and the lives of famous people. The tabloids are more popular than the broadsheets.

➔ *The Daily Mail* started in 1896 and it sells about 2,422,000 copies a day now. It costs 40 pence.

➔ *The Daily Express* started in 1900. It sells about 878,000 copies a day and costs 40 pence.

➔ *The Daily Mirror* started in 1903. It costs 35 pence and sells about 2,200,000 copies a day.

➔ *The Sun* is quite new – it started in 1964 – but it is really popular. It sells about 3,452,000 copies a day. It costs 30 pence.

---

b Read the text and answer the questions.

How do you know that newspapers are popular in Britain?

Because about 70 per cent of people read a newspaper every day.

1 What are the two types of newspaper?
_____, _____

2 Which type of newspaper has more news? _____

3 Which type of newspaper is more popular in Britain? _____

4 What is unusual about *The Guardian*?
_____
_____

2 Complete the table with information from the text.

	DATE STARTED	CIRCULATION	PRICE
The Daily Express	1900	878,000	40p
The Daily Mail			
The Daily Mirror			
The Daily Telegraph			
The Guardian			
The Independent			
The Sun			
The Times			

3 Find words and phrases with these meanings in the text.

1 an adjective from *nation* _____
2 a newspaper that isn't national _____
3 an adjective from *day* _____
4 news from around the world _____
5 the plural form of *life* _____

Grammar | comparison of adjectives

4 Use the table in Ex. 2 to compare the newspapers.

The Daily Mirror / The Sun / old
The Daily Mirror is older than The Sun.

The Independent / The Daily Telegraph / popular
The Daily Telegraph is more popular than The Independent.

1 *The Times / The Sun / cheap*

_____

_____

2 *The Guardian / The Daily Mail / expensive*

_____

_____

3 *The Daily Express / The Independent / new*

_____

_____

4 *The Daily Telegraph / The Daily Express / popular*

_____

_____

5 *The Daily Mail / The Guardian / old*

_____

_____

6 *The Daily Mirror / The Independent / cheap*

_____

_____

5 **a** Find nine more pairs of opposite adjectives.

> ~~formal~~ **tidy** **early**
>
> tight
>
> **hot** *untidy*
>
> **loose** *quiet*
>
> **unhealthy** **handsome**
>
> **smart**
>
> *noisy* ~~informal~~
>
> **easy** cold **difficult**
>
> casual *healthy* ugly

formal – informal   _____

_____   _____

_____   _____

_____   _____

b Choose pairs of adjectives from Ex. 5a to compare these people and things.

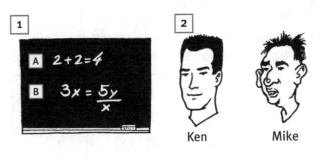

1
A 2 + 2 = 4
B 3x = 5y / x

2
Ken   Mike

3
living room

bedroom

4
Emma

Caroline

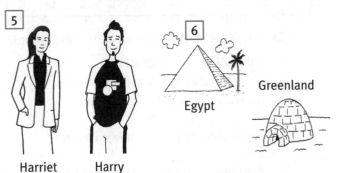

5
Harriet   Harry

6
Egypt   Greenland

1 *Sum A is easier than Sum B. / Sum B is more difficult than Sum A.*

2 _____

3 _____

4 _____

5 _____

6 _____

Pronunciation

6 **a** **9.1** Listen. Find the /ə/ sounds in these sentences and <u>underline</u> them.

Nov<u>e</u>ls <u>are</u> more popul<u>ar</u> th<u>a</u>n plays.

1 My brother is younger than me.

2 Fruit juice is nicer than water.

3 Newspapers are more versatile than TV.

4 Canada is colder than Brazil.

b Listen again and repeat.

Vocabulary | films

1 a Find seven more types of film in this word square. One type of film is two words in two places.

T	M	U	S	I	C	A	L	Y	D
A	G	S	C	I	E	N	C	E	F
R	D	T	Y	K	O	Q	H	W	I
D	F	V	A	B	J	X	O	S	C
C	O	M	E	D	Y	Z	R	G	T
W	C	M	L	N	T	U	R	O	I
E	D	C	A	R	T	O	O	N	O
F	T	X	E	T	S	U	R	N	N
L	O	V	E	S	T	O	R	Y	V
J	D	T	H	R	I	L	L	E	R

b Match the films from Ex. 1a to the descriptions.

It's a funny film.   a _comedy_

1   Girls and boys meet and fall in love. a _____

2   It's scary. Horrible things happen.
    a _____ film

3   The people aren't real. They're pictures.
    a _____

4   The story is exciting. There's lots of action.
    an _____ film

5   There's singing and dancing in this. a _____

6   People sometimes live on the stars in this type
    of film. a _____ film

7   You don't know the answer before the end.
    a _____

Grammar | superlative adjectives

2 All these sentences contain a mistake with the superlative. Correct the sentences.

Mr Sanders is the most rich man in our town.
the richest

1   Salima is the most best student in the class.
    _____

2   The Pacific is the bigger ocean in the world.
    _____

3   My sister's baby is newest member of our
    family. _____

4   I bought the most cheap printer in the shop.
    _____

5   Alicia is the most attractivest girl in the group.
    _____

3 Choose adjectives from the box to write sentences.

heavy   intelligent   ~~rich~~   romantic   tall   young

Martin has $30,000, Justin has $70,000 and Frank has $55,000.
Justin is the richest man.

1   Jane is 1m 90, Susan is 1m 73 and Maria is 1m 82.
    _____

2   Sarah's baby is three months old, Annabel's baby is four months old and Yvonne's baby is two months old.
    _____

3   Dave, Karin and Luis are all at university. Dave got 86 per cent in his exams, Karin got 74 per cent and Luis got 92 per cent.
    _____

4   Chris's weight is 72 kilos, Jan's weight is 67 kilos and Andreas's weight is 83 kilos.
    _____

5   Paul buys his girlfriend flowers on her birthday. William buys his girlfriend flowers every month. Peter buys his girlfriend flowers once a week.
    _____

4 a Write sentences using the prompts and _is, are, was_ or _were_.

rich / man / Bill Gates
The richest man is Bill Gates.

1   young / tennis champion / Martina Hingis
    _____
    _____

2   loud / rock band / The Who
    _____

3   noisy / plane / Concorde
    _____

4   dry / desert / the Atacama Desert in Chile
    _____

5   fast / animal / the cheetah
    _____

6   dangerous / roads / in India
    _____

b Write superlative sentences from the prompts, giving your opinions.

strange / animal *I think the strangest animal is the elephant.*

1 dangerous / animal

_____

2 handsome / actor

_____

3 untidy / person in my family

_____

4 good / singer or band

_____

5 boring / TV programme

_____

6 beautiful / place in my country

_____

Reading and writing

5 **a** Read the text and complete the 'review' column of the table.

One of my favourite books is Brazzaville Beach. It's by William Boyd, a British writer, and he wrote it in 1990. It's a thriller, but it's also a love story. It is set in Africa in the second half of the twentieth century. The main character is a woman called Hope Clearwater. She is studying chimpanzees and she notices that they can be very violent ... It's a very exciting and interesting book. Read it!

WILLIAM BOYD
brazzaville beach

b Look at the text again. Write the order of the information in the text.

the opinion of the writer	☐
information about the writer of the book	☐
information about the characters	☐
a few details about the story	☐
the name of the book	1
the location and time of the story	☐
the type of book	☐

6 **a** Complete the last column of the table with information about a book you like.

b Write a short review of your favourite book. Use Ex. 5 to help you, and the film review on page 89 of your Students' Book.

One of my favourite books is ...

	REVIEW	MY FAVOURITE BOOK
Name of book	*Brazzaville Beach*	
Name of writer	*William Boyd*	
Nationality of writer		
Date of writing		
Type of book		
Location (set in ...)		
Time of story (which year)		
Main character		
Main event(s)		
Adjectives to describe book		

Listening

1 a **9.2** Cover the tapescript. Listen to an information service for St Petersburg. Put the places in the order you hear them (1–5).

a   Mussorgsky Theatre ☐
b   Smolny Institute ☐
c   Hermitage Museum ☐ 1
d   Mariinsky Theatre ☐
e   Russian Museum ☐

b Listen again and match the places in Ex. 1a to the exhibitions and events in the box.

> modern Russian sculpture ☐   *Swan Lake* ☐
> Impressionist paintings ☐ c   abstract art ☐
> *The Marriage of Figaro* ☐

c Answer the questions. Listen again or read the tapescript to check your answers.

1   Where can you see paintings by Monet?

_____

2   Where can you see paintings by Malevich?

_____

3   What can you buy at the Mariinsky Theatre box office?

_____

4   What time does the Mariinsky Theatre box office open?

_____

5   When is the performance of *The Marriage of Figaro*?

_____

> **EXERCISE 1 TAPESCRIPT**
>
> Welcome to the St Petersburg English Language Tourist Information Line. This week we have a number of cultural events and special exhibitions taking place in the city. At the Hermitage Museum, there is an exhibition of Impressionist paintings including works by Cézanne and Monet. At the Smolny Institute, there is an exhibition of abstract art, including paintings by Malevich. If you prefer sculpture, there is an exhibition of modern Russian sculpture at the Russian Museum.
>
> For ballet lovers, the Kirov Ballet is performing *Swan Lake* at the Mariinsky Theatre this week. You can buy tickets for *Swan Lake* at the Mariinsky Theatre box office which is open from 11.00 a.m. to 7.00 p.m. every day. If you prefer going to the opera, there is a performance of *The Marriage of Figaro* at the Mussorgsky Opera and Ballet Theatre on Wednesday. You can buy tickets for the Mussorgsky Theatre at the box office between ...

Grammar | *prefer*

2 Tick (✓) the sentence (a or b) with the same meaning as the first sentence.

1   I like Jane more than Julie.
    a   I prefer Julie to Jane. ☐
    b   I prefer Jane to Julie. ☐
2   We think art is more interesting than music.
    a   We prefer art to music. ☐
    b   We prefer music to art. ☐
3   Do you like beef more than chicken?
    a   Do you prefer beef to chicken? ☐
    b   Do you prefer chicken to beef? ☐

3 Tick (✓) the words we can use to complete the sentences.

1   I prefer ... to tea.
    a   drink coffee ☐   b   coffee ☐
    c   of coffee ☐
2   I like novels but my brother prefers ... newspapers.
    a   read ☐   b   reading ☐
    c   reads ☐
3   Samuel prefers cars ... motorbikes.
    a   of ☐   b   than ☐
    c   to ☐
4   Does he ... playing tennis?
    a   prefer swimming ☐   b   prefer swim to ☐
    c   prefer swimming to ☐
5   I usually prefer ....
    a   read than write ☐   b   reading to writing ☐
    c   read to write ☐

4 Rewrite the sentences using *prefer*.

I like Monet more than Picasso.

I prefer Monet to Picasso.

She thinks drinking water is better than drinking fruit juice.

She prefers drinking water to drinking fruit juice.

1 Dario likes traditional art more than modern art.

_____
_____
_____

2 The children are more interested in playing than in reading.

_____
_____
_____

3 I think action films are more exciting than horror films.

_____
_____
_____

4 Clara watches television more than she listens to music.

_____
_____
_____

5 We hardly ever visit museums but we often go to concerts.

_____
_____
_____

6 I like Italian food but my favourite food is French.

_____
_____
_____

Grammar | *will* for spontaneous decisions and offers

5 Write responses using *will* + a verb from the box and the expression in brackets.

> check   phone   get   go   ~~answer~~   look at   ask   open

There's someone at the door. (it) *I'll answer it.*

1 Where is the post office? (the map)

_____

2 Can we meet at seven o'clock? (in my diary)

_____

3 I can't open the door. (the key)

_____

4 Does your husband want to come? (him)

_____

5 She's very sick. (the doctor)

_____

6 It's very hot in here. (the window)

_____

7 We need some milk. (to the supermarket)

_____

6 Correct the mistakes in the offers (1–4). Then match them to the pictures (A–D).

		correction	picture
1	I'll to get the instructions.	_____	☐
2	I get it for you.	_____	☐
3	I will gave you a refund.	_____	☐
4	I'll turning on the lights.	_____	☐

Grammar

Possessive pronouns; *one/ones*

1 In each sentence, find a place where it is better to use a pronoun than a noun or noun phrase. Underline the noun (phrase) and write the correct pronoun.

I love apples, especially red <u>apples</u>. *ones*

This is your coffee and this is <u>my coffee</u>. *mine*

1 The party isn't at my parents' house; it's at our house. _____

2 This isn't your wallet; it's my wallet. _____

3 Those flowers are lovely, especially the pink flowers. _____

4 'Which is the bus for the centre?' 'The bus on the right.' _____

5 'Is this their house?' 'No, the one with the blue door is their house.' _____

6 'Is this your bag?' 'No, it's your bag!' _____

Past Simple: irregular verbs

2 Complete the sentences with the correct form of the verbs in the box.

> buy   have   not keep   leave   see   spend

1 _____ you _____ the TV news last night?

2 We _____ a lot of money on clothes last weekend.

3 Penny _____ work at five o'clock yesterday.

4 We _____ pizza for dinner yesterday.

5 Allie and Jake _____ a new car last week.

6 'Have you got the receipt?' 'No, sorry. I _____ it.'

Adverbs of frequency

3 Write the correct adverb of frequency for the underlined phrase. Then rewrite the sentence.

I see my niece about <u>four times a year</u>. *sometimes*
I see my niece sometimes.

1 I get up early <u>every day</u>. _____
_____

2 We go to the cinema on Friday evenings <u>almost every week</u>. _____
_____

3 I watch football <u>about once a year</u>. _____
_____

4 I <u>don't</u> drink coffee after 6.oo in the evening.
_____
_____

Present Continuous

4 Write sentences in the Present Continuous.

What / Jean / wear / today?
What is Jean wearing today?

Andy / not / study / this evening
Andy isn't studying this evening.

1 Dan and Gemma / make / a Chinese meal
_____
_____

2 What / Steve / do / in the garden?
_____

3 Laura / wear / a long skirt / this evening
_____
_____

4 What / you / watch / on TV?
_____

5 Mum / not / speak / to Dad at the moment
_____
_____

6 The boys / play / tennis in the park
_____
_____

7 Our daughter / sleep / in her room
_____

8 Where / you / plan / to go on holiday?
_____

9 I / not / have / anything to eat
_____

10 What / you / carry / in that bag?
_____

Present Simple and Continuous

5 Choose the correct form of the verb.

Hi Emily

How are you? I *send / am sending* this email to ask if you are busy this afternoon. If not, can you come to my apartment for coffee? As you know, Gerry and I (1) *usually work / are usually working* during the day and we (2) *don't get home / aren't getting home* before six in the evening, but today I (3) *have / am having* a day at home. I (4) *wait / am waiting* for a new cooker! We bought it on Saturday and it (5) *comes / is coming* today – I hope! The shop (6) *brings / is bringing* it some time today, but I don't know when exactly. Our old cooker broke last week, and we need a new cooker because we both (7) *enjoy / are enjoying* cooking. Gerry and I (8) *cook / are cooking* every evening, so it's very difficult without a cooker. So (9) *do you do / are you doing* anything today?

Love
Karen

Adverbs of manner

6 Complete the sentences with adverbs of manner.

That was careless. → You did that _carelessly_ .

1 Sue's a fast driver. → She drives
_____.

2 That's a noisy game. → They're playing
_____.

3 We have a healthy diet. → We eat
_____.

4 That was a good match. → You played
_____.

5 Tony wears casual clothes. → He dresses
_____.

6 It was an easy exercise. → We did it
_____.

7 She's a very quiet speaker. → She speaks very
_____.

8 Is that sofa comfortable? → Are you sitting
_____?

9 He's very careful when he chooses clothes. →
He chooses clothes _____.

10 Kevin is a slow worker. → He works
_____.

Comparison of adjectives

7 Write sentences using comparative and superlative adjectives and the information below.

	AGE	HEIGHT	WEIGHT
Joe	33	1.80m	82kg
Ian	26	1.85m	75kg
Mac	40	1.95m	80kg

Joe / Ian – short _Joe is shorter than Ian._
Joe / Ian / Mac – old _Mac is the oldest._

1 Ian / Mac – heavy _____
_____

2 Joe / Mac – old _____
_____

3 Joe / Ian / Mac – tall _____

4 Joe / Mac – short _____
_____

5 Joe / Ian / Mac – young _____

6 Joe / Ian – heavy _____
_____

7 Joe / Ian / Mac – short _____

8 Ian / Mac – young _____
_____

9 Joe / Ian – old _____
_____

10 Joe / Ian / Mac – heavy _____

Prefer + noun/-ing form

8 Six of these sentences have mistakes.
Tick (✓) the two correct sentences and correct the sentences with mistakes.

1 We prefer old films than modern films. ☐
_____

2 I prefer white wine to red wine. ☐
_____

3 Matt prefers play football to play badminton. ☐
_____

4 We're preferring fish to meat for dinner. ☐
_____

5 She's prefer opera to ballet. ☐
_____

6 Do you prefer swim or sunbathe? ☐
_____

7 Kate prefers cycling to work to taking the bus. ☐

8 I prefer doing roleplays than doing grammar exercises. ☐
_____

Vocabulary

9 **a** Underline the odd one out.

1 foggy   windy   pretty
2 thriller   ballet   cartoon
3 tight   trainers   trousers
4 novel   pullover   poetry
5 first   sixteenth   slim
6 comedy   impressionist   abstract
7 suit   hat   hot
8 belt   formal   smart

b Complete the sentences with the underlined words from Exercise 9a.

1 I need to wear a _____ because my trousers are loose.

2 It's always _____ in the Mediterranean in summer.

3 Alison is very _____ now – she lost a lot of weight last year.

4 I don't like any kind of dancing so I don't like _____.

5 Put your _____ on – it's very cold today.

6 Everyone likes _____ films when they feel sad, because they laugh and feel better.

7 This skirt is _____ – can I try a bigger size, please?

8 Cathy is small, fair and very _____.

Vocabulary | travel and holiday activities

1 **a** <u>Underline</u> the odd one out in each list.

1 garage   drive   car   underground train
2 train   flight   station   platform
3 cycling   hiking   park   bungee jumping
4 commuting   rush hour   long-haul   traffic
5 passenger   ticket   plane   bicycle

b Use words from Ex. 1a to complete the gaps.

1 The train to the airport leaves from _____ 6.
2 It is always difficult to _____ a car in the centre of big cities.
3 _____ flights are quite expensive.
4 My parents gave me a _____ for my tenth birthday.
5 I've got a car so I need a house with a _____.

Listening

2 **a** [10.1] Listen to an extract from a job interview. What is the job?

b Listen again. Tick (✓) the places Della has been to and cross (✗) the places she hasn't been to.

1 New York ☐   5 Singapore ☐
2 Washington ☐   6 Sydney ☐
3 Rio de Janeiro ☐ 7 San Antonio ☐
4 Bangkok ☐   8 Rimini ☐

c Listen again and write when she went to three of the places in Ex. 2b.

Grammar | Present Perfect *been* with *ever/never: I, we, you, they*

3 Read the questions and write the answers for Della. Then write true answers for you.

1 Have you ever been on a package holiday?
Della: *Yes, I have.*
You: _____

2 Have you ever been on an adventure holiday?
Della: _____
You: _____

3 Have you ever been to any holiday resorts?
Della: _____
You: _____

4 **a** Complete each gap with one word from the box. You can use each word more than once.

> been   've   have   haven't   ever   never   went

Int 1: So, Della. Tell us about your travel experiences.
Della: Well, I *'ve* been to lots of different places around the world.
Int 1: Where exactly have you (1) been?
Della: I've been to New York and Washington. And I (2) _____ to Rio de Janeiro last winter.
Int 1: What about Asia? (3) have you been to Bangkok?
Della: No, I've (4) _____ been there. But I've been to Singapore.
Int 1: What about Sydney?
Della: Er, no. I (5) have been there.
Int 2: That's all very interesting, but have you (6) ever been to any holiday resorts?
Della: Yes, I've been to San Antonio, in Ibiza. And I've been to Rimini, in Italy.
Int 2: When did you go there?
Della: Well, I went to Rimini when I was at university. And I (7) _____ to San Antonio last summer.
Int 2: Was that a package holiday?
Della: Yes, it was.
Int 1: Have you (8) _____ on any adventure holidays?
Della: No, I (9) _____.
Int 2: So, why do you want to be a holiday rep?
Della: Well, there was a holiday rep at the resort in San Antonio. She was really good. That's the reason I applied for this job!

b Listen again and check your answers.

5 Look at the prompts and write Present Perfect positive (✓) sentences, negative (✗) sentences or questions (?).

We / to Canada (✓)
We've been to Canada.
I / horse-riding (✗)
I haven't been horse-riding.
You / on a long-haul flight (?)
Have you been on a long-haul flight?

1 I / bungee jumping (✓)

2 We / to Bangkok (✗)

3 you / to London (?)

4 they / on a package holiday (?)

5 John and Julie / to Australia (✗)

6 I / on an adventure holiday (✗)

7 Our parents / to Florida (✓)

8 you / to an IMAX cinema (?)

9 We / hiking in the mountains (✓)

10 your cousins / to your new house (?)

6 Match the sentence halves.

1	Have you ever been	a	go there last year?
2	Yes, they went there	b	there twice.
3	Yes, I've been	c	I haven't.
4	No,	d	to Greece?
5	Yes,	e	been there.
6	Did you	f	in 2004.
7	No, I haven't	g	I have.

7 Write questions with *Have you ever* and write true answers about you.

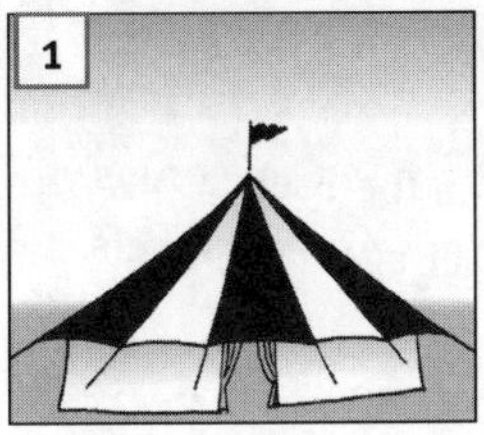

Have you ever been to a circus?
No, I haven't. / Yes, I have.
I went last year.

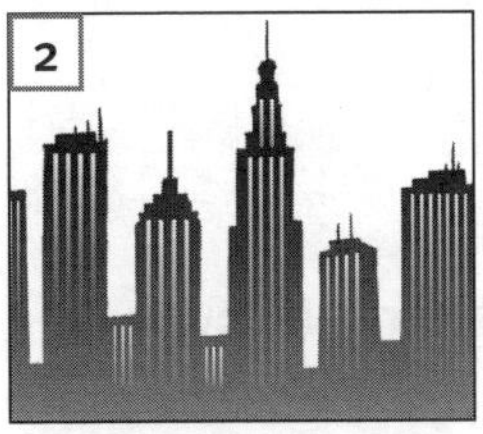

Pronunciation

8 **a** [10.2] Listen to the underlined sounds A and B in the examples. Circle the correct symbol for each sound.

      A B
Have you ev<u>e</u>r b<u>ee</u>n to England?

      B A
Yes, I've b<u>ee</u>n t<u>o</u> London.

A = /ɪ/ or /ə/?
B = /ɪ/ or /ə/?

b [10.3] Listen to the underlined sound in each sentence and tick (✓) the correct box.

	/ɪ/	/ə/
1 I've nev<u>e</u>r been there.	☐	☐
2 Have you b<u>ee</u>n to Australia?	☐	☐
3 We've b<u>ee</u>n bungee jumping.	☐	☐
4 Have you been on <u>a</u> horse?	☐	☐
5 Have you been to <u>I</u>taly?	☐	☐
6 Have you been t<u>o</u> Madrid?	☐	☐

Vocabulary | holidays

1 Match the extracts from postcards below with the types of holiday.

> activity   beach   cultural   water sports
> winter sports   sightseeing

1. Jason has tried sailing and windsurfing and tomorrow ... _____

2. We've visited all the museums and have been to the famous ballet. _____

3. I've found this fantastic little beach with no people ... _____

4. We've played golf and tennis ... _____

5. I'm really tired. I've walked for hours in the city today. _____

6. Serena has spent every day skiing. _____

b Which holiday is the best for these people? Write the places.

1. My friends and I want to go on holiday in the summer. We're all eighteen or nineteen and we like the sun. We want to have a good time! _____

2. Stephen and I want to get away for a few nights. We don't like the sun and we don't want to be active. We belong to a classical music club. _____

3. My girlfriend wants to go on holiday during the winter, but we're not sure what kind of holiday. We don't want to stay in a city, but a beach in the winter isn't a good idea. We don't ski, so that's a problem. _____

3 In which place or places can you do these things?

1. stay in a hotel _____
2. travel to the place by road _____
3. take lessons _____
4. enjoy a busy nightlife _____
5. stay in an apartment _____
6. go swimming _____

Reading

2 **a** Look at the texts. Which three types of holiday do they describe?

1. _____

Verona opera season
Short breaks for opera lovers

Plan your own short holiday in one of Italy's most romantic cities. Travel by air or road and stay in a three-star city-centre hotel for two, three or four nights. The price includes:

- travel to Verona
- bed and breakfast in city-centre hotel
- a ticket to one opera

2. _____

CRETE'S HOTTEST RESORT

Agios Nikolaos is one of Crete's busiest and most popular resorts, with lots of sandy beaches for swimming and sunbathing. It also has the best nightlife on the island with lots of restaurants and bars, plus nightclubs for all ages. Our fabulous four-star hotel has all the facilities you need: two restaurants, bars, a health studio and gym, two swimming pools, a private beach, shops and a beauty salon.

3. _____

Les Arcs

One of France's best-known resorts, high in the French Alps, Les Arcs offers something for skiers of all ages and levels, even for non-skiers.

You can stay in the main hotel or in an apartment, where you can cook your own meals or take your meals in one of the first-class restaurants at the resort.

For experienced skiers there are pistes of all levels of difficulty. If this is your first time skiing, or if you haven't skied for a long time, there are classes at all levels.

Grammar | Present Perfect with regular and irregular verbs

4 Write about people on the holidays in Ex. 2a. Use the words in brackets and write a positive or a negative sentence.

Saskia is on holiday in Les Arcs.

(go to the beach) (✗) _Saskia hasn't been to the beach._

(learn to ski) (✓) _She's learnt to ski._

1 (cook all her meals) (✗)

_____

2 (visit the sights) (✓)

_____

Pawel is on holiday in Verona.

3 (see an opera) (✓)

_____

4 (learn to ski) (✗)

_____

5 (go on a city tour) (✓)

_____

Karl and Tara are on holiday in Agios Nikolaos.

6 (have a quiet week) (✗)

_____

7 (go to lots of nightclubs) (✓)

_____

8 (spend hours on the beach) (✓)

_____

Lifelong learning | record past participles

5 **a** Complete the table with the past participles.

	INFINITIVE	PAST PARTICIPLE
1	become	_____
2	catch	_____
3	drive	_____
4	forget	_____
5	keep	_____
6	meet	_____
7	ride	_____
8	wear	_____

b Complete the sentences with a verb from the table in the Present Perfect.

1 _____ you ever _____ a horse?

2 Oh no! I _____ my key!

3 I _____ never _____ this jumper.

4 _____ you _____ my friend Aileen?

5 Gerald _____ an enormous fish!

6 Your son _____ very tall now he's older.

7 My brother _____ a Ferrari.

8 _____ your parents _____ photos of you when you were a child?

Pronunciation

6 **a** Underline the word with the long vowel in each pair.

1 a) cat   b) car

2 a) fill   b) feel

3 a) taught   b) top

4 a) am   b) arm

5 a) heart   b) hat

6 a) cost   b) course

b **10.4** Listen and check, then practise the pairs.

Writing

7 **a** Choose one of the places in Ex. 2. You are on holiday there. Make notes to answer the questions.

1 Where are you staying? (hotel/apartment)

_____

2 What is it like?

_____

3 What is the resort like?

_____

4 What has the weather been like?

_____

5 Who are you with?

_____

6 What have you done? What has your friend (wife, etc.) done?

_____

b Write a postcard to a friend in your notebook. Use your notes and the Writing Bank on page 143 of your Students' Book.

Reading

http://www.technologyreview.co.uk/

Technology*review*

Search

[Products] [GO]

Citybug electric scooter

Star rating ★★★☆☆

Commuting in big cities is getting more and more *difficult*. You can't park cars. Buses are slow. Trains are expensive and crowded. What can you do?

Cycling is the answer for many people. It's *great* if your city streets are flat and you are fit and have lots of energy. But many people get tired and it's very difficult to cycle up *hills*.

So, if you want to find an easy way to commute and you don't have a lot of energy, try the Citybug electric *scooter*.

The Citybug has an electric engine with a *top speed* of 14 miles per hour (22 kilometres per hour). It loves going up hills!

Because the Citybug is electric you don't need to go to the *petrol station*! You just *connect* the Citybug to the electricity in your house for one or two hours. So it's very cheap.

Riding the Citybug is easy, but the seat and the wheels are small, so it isn't very comfortable. Of course it isn't fast, and it weighs 21 kg so it's quite heavy. But it's easy to park and you don't need a driving licence, so adults or children can use it.

[Check] our price comparison page for the latest prices.

---

1 a Where is the text from? Read it and choose the correct answer, A, B or C.

A a newspaper ☐

B a magazine ☐

C an Internet page ☐

b Read the text again. Match these explanations to the words and expressions in italics in the text.

small mountains *hills*

1 a place where you can buy petrol for your car

_____

2 the fastest speed _____

3 not easy _____

4 look at _____

5 small motorbike _____

6 join two things together _____

7 very good _____

c Write notes in the table.

The Citybug electric scooter	
ADVANTAGES	**DISADVANTAGES**
You don't need a lot of energy.	*It isn't very fast.*

Vocabulary | travel and transport (VB p85)

2 Match 1–7 to a–g to make phrases.

1	one-way	a	hour
2	long-haul	b	class
3	economy	c	date
4	underground	d	agent
5	rush	e	train
6	departure	f	ticket
7	travel	g	flight

3 Use expressions from Ex. 2 to complete the sentences.

1 I go to work on an _____ because it's fast and efficient.

2 Tuesday 15th October. Is that your _____?

3 I don't want to come back so I need a _____.

4 Sometimes the seats in _____ on a flight are very small and uncomfortable.

5 In New York the morning _____ is between 7.00 and 9.00a.m.

Grammar | -ing form

4 Write sentences from the prompts using the -ing form. Use an adjective from the box to complete each sentence.

> relaxing expensive scary easy dangerous difficult healthy exciting

send / text messages
Sending text messages is easy.

1 watch / horror films
_____

2 eat / lots of fruit and vegetables
_____

3 drive / in fog
_____

4 learn / a foreign language
_____

5 swim / in warm water
_____

6 visit / new places
_____

7 fly / in business class
_____

5 Rewrite the sentences using the -ing form.

It's cheap to travel by underground in Paris.
Travelling by underground is cheap in Paris.

1 It's difficult to park a car in big cities.
_____

2 It's easy to get information from the Internet.
_____

3 It's romantic to send flowers to your wife or girlfriend.
_____

4 It's nice to get an email from your best friend.
_____

5 It's interesting to watch the news on TV.
_____

How to ... | book a travel ticket

6 **a** Read the dialogue and complete 1–6 with a suitable word.

Stephen: Do you sell airline (1) _____ for Brazil? We'd like two tickets from Amsterdam (2) _____ Rio de Janeiro.

Travel agent: OK. What is your departure date?

Stephen: a) *Saturday the 21st.*

Travel agent: One (3) _____ or return?

Stephen: b) _____

Travel agent: Business class or (4) _____ class?

Stephen: c) _____

Travel agent: Let me see ... We have a (5) _____ with Varig.

Stephen: d) _____

Travel agent: It's €650.

Stephen: e) _____

Travel agent: No, it (6) _____ in Lisbon.

Stephen: f) _____

Travel agent: It leaves Amsterdam at 10.30 in the morning.

b Write the sentences from the box in the gaps a–f in the conversation in Ex.6a.

> How much is that flight? Is it a direct flight? Economy class, please. ~~Saturday the 21st.~~ Return. We'd like to come back on Saturday the 28th. What time does it leave?

c **10.5** Listen and check your answers.

Reading

1 **a** Read the notice quickly and choose the best answer, A, B or C.

The notice gives:

A information and advice
B information and rules
C advice

b Match the highlighted words in the text to the pictures.

1 _____

3 _____

2 _____

4 _____

c Match 1–5 to their meanings a–e. (The words are in the same order as in the text.)

1 proof ☐
2 the hold ☐
3 hand luggage ☐
4 checked luggage ☐
5 boarding ☐

a The bags you give in at the check-in desk.
b Entering a plane.
c This is the place on a plane where they put the bags.
d This shows that something is true.
e Small bags <u>you</u> take on the plane.

Sunshine Holidays

If you are flying with *Go Faster Airlines* please read this notice before you go to the airport.

Documents

Go Faster Airlines uses an electronic check-in system. You don't have to bring your tickets to the check-in desk, but you have to bring proof of your identity (including your photo): for example a passport, driving licence or identity card.
If you are flying to another country, you have to show your passport.

Luggage

With *Go Faster Airlines* you can check in a maximum of 20kg of luggage to put in the hold. You can take a maximum of 5kg of hand luggage. You can't put **sharp objects** in your hand luggage. You have to put them in your checked luggage. Your suitcase has to have a label with your name and address. The label doesn't have to have your flight number because that is on the electronic label.

Electronic devices

You have to switch off all electronic devices before boarding the plane.
You can't use your mobile phone inside the plane.

Grammar | *can/can't, have to/don't have to*

2 Read the notice in Ex. 1 again. Tick (✓) the correct columns in the table.

	NECESSARY	NOT NECESSARY	POSSIBLE	NOT POSSIBLE
1 bring tickets to the check-in desk		✓		
2 bring proof of your identity				
3 show your passport when you fly to another country				
4 check in 20kg of luggage				
5 take more than 5kg of hand luggage				
6 put sharp objects in your hand luggage				
7 put a label on your suitcase with your name and address				
8 put your flight number on your suitcase label				
9 switch off electronic devices before you board the plane				
10 use a mobile phone inside the plane				

3 Use these airport rules to write two sentences with *can't* and three sentences with *have to*.

> ### Rules
> - Be at check-in two hours before your departure time.
> - ~~No smoking on the plane.~~
> - Don't take drinks onto the plane.
> - Turn off your mobile phone before you board the plane.
> - Don't take food on the plane.
> - Wear your seat belt during the flight.

can't

You can't smoke on the plane.

1 _____

_____

2 _____

_____

have to

3 _____

_____

4 _____

_____

5 _____

_____

4 Complete the sentences using a form of *have to, don't have to, can* or *can't*.

It isn't necessary to wear a suit in my office.

I *don't have to wear a suit in my office.*

In New York, people aren't allowed to smoke in restaurants.

You *can't smoke in restaurants in New York.*

1 It isn't possible to drive a car when you are only fifteen years old.

You _____

_____.

2 Bring a friend to the party if you want to.

I _____

_____.

3 In my office it isn't possible to use our mobile phones.

We _____

_____.

4 Show your receipt to the manager.

You _____

_____.

5 There's no parking near the theatre.

You _____

_____.

6 It isn't necessary for Amanda to pay because she's a member of the club.

Amanda _____

_____.

7 We accept payment by cash or credit card.

You _____

_____.

8 It isn't necessary for David and Lucy to get visas to go to Canada.

David and Lucy _____

_____.

Vocabulary | road rules and signs

5 Complete the sentences with words or expressions from the box.

> seat belt   fine   traffic lights   turn right
> offence   driving licence   obey   driving test

1 There are three colours on _____:
red, yellow and green.

2 It is an _____ to go faster than the speed limit.

3 In most countries drivers have to wear a _____.

4 I'm a good driver. I haven't got any points on my _____.

5 Did you pass your _____?

6 I paid a €75 _____ because I drove faster than the speed limit.

7 Do you always _____ the rules of the road?

8 In the USA you can _____ at a red traffic light.

Pronunciation

6 **a** `11.1` In this sentence there are two /f/ sounds and two /v/ sounds. Listen and <u>underline</u> one more /f/ sound and one more /v/ sound. Write the correct sound above them.

/f/   /v/
You don't have to have a French visa.

b `11.2` Listen and tick (✓) the correct box.

	/f/	/v/
1 I have to go home now.	☐	☐
2 Do you have a car?	☐	☐
3 I've got a question.	☐	☐
4 Let's have a drink tomorrow.	☐	☐
5 Do you have to leave now?	☐	☐

Listening

1 `11.3` Cover the tapescript. Listen to three interviews. Write the number of the interview by the correct person.

☐ an American Maths teacher

☐ an American woman in her thirties

☐ an older English man, he didn't like school

☐ a young man, he didn't go to university

☐ a teacher of French and Spanish

2 **a** Tick (✓) the correct interview.

Which person or people …	1	2	3
1 liked Maths and Geography?	☐	☐	☐
2 left school quite early?	☐	☐	☐
3 didn't go to university?	☐	☐	☐
4 enjoyed languages at school?	☐	☐	☐
5 got married in England?	☐	☐	☐

b Complete the table for interviews 2 and 3.

	1	2	3
1 Age started school?	5		
2 Location of school?	London		
3 Time spent at school?	9 years		
4 Enjoyed school?	no		
5 Favourite subject(s)?	sport		
6 Went to university?	no		

EXERCISES 1 AND 2 TAPESCRIPT

1

A: Excuse me, can I ask you some questions about your schooldays?

B: You can, but it was a long time ago!

A: When did you start school?

B: When I was about five, I think. Yes, I was five.

A: And where did you go to school?

B: In London. I was in London through all my years at school.

A: How long did you stay at school?

B: Oh, only about nine years, I think. Yes, I left school when I was fourteen.

A: Did you enjoy school?

B: No, I hated it.

A: What was your favourite subject?

B: I didn't have one … well, I suppose it was sport.

A: Did you go to university?

B: Oh, no. I left school and I went to work. I wanted some money!

2

A: Excuse me, can I ask you some questions about your schooldays?

B: Yes, sure.

A: When did you start school?

B: When I was six.

A: And where did you go to school?

B: In Texas. I'm from the USA, so I went to school there.

A: How long did you stay at school?

B: From six to eighteen, so, what's that? Twelve years.

A: Did you enjoy school?

B: Yeah, it was OK.

A: What was your favourite subject?

B: I liked Maths and Geography. I wasn't very good at English.

A: Did you go to university?

B: Well, I started college – I started studying Maths, but I didn't really enjoy it, so I left. Then I came here, to England, and I met my husband, and, well, that's it!

3

A: Excuse me, can I ask you some questions about your schooldays?

B: Yes, of course.

A: When did you start school?

B: Oh, the usual age, five, I think.

A: And where did you go to school?

B: In Scotland.

A: How long did you stay at school?

B: Er, until I was eighteen, so about thirteen years in total.

A: Did you enjoy school?

B: Yes, I did. I really liked it.

A: What was your favourite subject?

B: I loved languages – French and Spanish.

A: Did you go to university?

B: Yes, I finished university two years ago – I studied French and Spanish there, too, and now I'm teaching French and Spanish and I really enjoy it!

Grammar | review of *wh-* questions

3 **a** Write the questions that the interviewer asked. Use the prompts in the table in Ex. 2b to help you. (Not all the questions need a *wh-* word.)

When did you start school?

1 _____
2 _____
3 _____
4 _____
5 _____

b Check your answers in the tapescript for Ex. 1 and 2.

4 **a** Look at the groups of questions. Write the correct *wh-* word from the box in each group.

> how   how many   what   when   where   ~~which~~
> who   why

Which subjects did you do? / school did you go to? / teacher do you like best?

1 _____ students are there in your class? / languages can you speak? / subjects have you got on Monday?

2 _____ do you sit next to? / is your favourite film star? / do you live with?

3 _____ is the school? / is your house? / do you go in the evenings?

4 _____ time is it? / do you do at the weekend? / did you watch on TV yesterday?

5 _____ do you get to the school? / do you spend your holidays? / did you find this school?

6 _____ do you get up? / did you start learning English? / do you take exercise?

7 _____ are you learning English? / do you live in the city? / did you say that?

b Find the correct question from Ex. 4a for each answer.

1 *Where do you go in the evenings?*
We often go to a bar or to the cinema.

2 _____
Two years ago.

3 _____
My parents and my younger brother.

4 _____
I take the bus.

5 _____
I went to Kingston High School.

6 _____
A programme about the Sahara desert.

7 _____
Because I need it for my job.

8 _____
Three – Physics, Maths and English.

c Make the answers in Ex. 4b true for you.

1 _____
2 _____
3 _____
4 _____
5 _____
6 _____
7 _____
8 _____

Pronunciation

5 **a** **11.4** Look at the questions you wrote in Ex. 3a. Does the voice go up or down in the questions? Listen and write ↗ or ↘ by each question.

When did you start school? ↘

b Now repeat the questions.

Writing

6 **a** Make notes to answer these questions about learning English in your country.

1 When do children start learning English?
2 Is English the first or second foreign language?
3 Is it a compulsory or optional subject?
4 How many years do they learn English at school?
5 Which parts of the language are most important at school (grammar, reading ...)?
6 What English exams do they take? When?
7 Can people study English when they leave school? Where?
8 Why do people usually study English after they finish school?

b Match the questions from Ex. 6a with the topics. Write the numbers.

English at school: *1* _____
English after school: _____
What we study: _____

c Write a short account of English studies in your country. Choose one of the options.

1 Write three paragraphs based on the topics in Ex. 6b. (Decide on the best order.)
2 Write one paragraph about learning English after leaving school.

Grammar | Present Continuous for future

1 **a** Cristina left university two weeks ago, and she's very busy. Look at her diary for this week and answer the questions with full sentences.

Monday July 12th	Thursday July 15th
travel to London a.m. [Regent Hotel] prepare for interview p.m.	bank manager 2.00p.m.
Tuesday July 13th	Friday July 16th
interview for job 9.30a.m. train back home 1.00p.m.	swimming with Dave 9.00a.m. driving test 4.30p.m.
Wednesday July 14th	Saturday July 17th
start summer day school 10.00a.m.	shopping with Alison 11.30a.m. Bailey's nightclub 10.00p.m., with Keira
	Sunday July 18th
	lunch with Mum and Dad 1.30p.m.

Is Cristina travelling to London on Monday?

Yes, she's travelling to London on Monday morning.

Is she having an interview for a university place on Tuesday?

No, she's having an interview for a job on Tuesday.

1 Is she catching the train home on Tuesday morning?

_____

_____

2 Is she starting an evening class on Wednesday?

_____

_____

3 Is she seeing the bank manager on Thursday?

_____

4 Is she taking her driving test on Friday morning?

_____

5 Is she going to the cinema with Keira on Saturday?

_____

_____

6 Is she going to her mum and dad's on Sunday?

_____

_____

b Write questions about Cristina using the prompts. Then write short answers.

stay / at the Regent Hotel / in London

Is Cristina staying at the Regent Hotel in London?
Yes, she is.

What / do / on Monday afternoon

What is she doing on Monday afternoon?
Preparing for the job interview.

1 have / the interview / on Tuesday morning

_____

_____

2 What time / catch / the train / on Tuesday

_____

_____

3 When / meet / the bank manager

_____

_____

4 go swimming / with Dave / Friday

_____

_____

5 go shopping / on Saturday afternoon

_____

_____

6 Who / Cristina / go shopping / with

_____

_____

Vocabulary | education

2 **a** Write one word from the box under each heading.

> degree Physics pupil
> secondary school trainer

educational institutions	qualifications	people studying	people teaching	school subjects

b Add at least one more word for each heading.

3 Choose the correct adjective to complete each sentence.

1 In my school we have to do one foreign language but the second one is *compulsory / optional*.

2 I want to be a car mechanic so I'm doing *an academic /a vocational* qualification at college.

3 I can't afford to stop working so I'm taking a *full-time /part-time* course on two evenings a week.

4 My parents sent me to a *private /state* school because we didn't have a lot of money.

5 I enjoy studying at home on my own, so a *classroom-learning /distance-learning* course is very good for me.

How to ... | talk about future arrangements

4 Write the sentences in the How to ... table.

~~Let's say Tuesday evening at 7.00.~~
What are you and Paula doing on Friday evening?
Let's put it in our diaries.
We're taking Paula's niece to the cinema.
Why don't you come to us on Saturday, then?
~~I'm afraid that's impossible.~~
Can you come at four o'clock?
I'm afraid we can't come then.
~~How about early Tuesday evening?~~

HOW TO ...	
ask about plans	
express an arrangement	
suggest a time	
refuse politely	*I'm afraid that's impossible.*
suggest an alternative	*How about early Tuesday evening?*
make an arrangement	*Let's say Tuesday evening at 7.00.*

5 **a** Complete the dialogues with the sentences from Ex. 4.

1 A: Excuse me, can I make an appointment to see you about our son's schoolwork?

B: Of course. I'm free on Friday afternoon. *Can you come at four o'clock?*

A: Oh, I'm sorry, (1) _____ _____. My husband's working on Friday afternoon.

B: So, are evenings better?

A: Yes, they are.

B: OK, (2) _____ _____? I always stay late at school then.

A: Yes, that's fine.

B: Good. (3) _____ _____.

A: OK. Thank you.

2 A: Hi Tony, (4) _____ _____?

B: Friday evening? (5) _____ _____ Why?

A: We're having some friends to dinner and wanted to ask you.

B: Well, (6) _____ _____ – we've got the tickets.

A: Oh, don't worry. (7) _____ _____

B: That's great – are you sure?

A: Of course! (8) _____ _____ – half past seven on Saturday.

B: Fine. See you then.

b 11.5 Listen and check your answers.

Reading

1 Complete the postcard with words and expressions from the box. You don't need all the words and expressions.

> tunnel   white-water rafting   island   trekking
> continent   coast   sailing   canyon

Listening

2   **a** **12.1** Listen. What is the connection between the photo and the map?

b Listen again and put Anthony's intentions in the correct order (1–7).

go trekking in the Rocky Mountains	☐
stay in Seattle	☐
fly home	☐
drive to the American border	☐
stay with his cousins	☐
fly to Vancouver	1
go to Whistler	☐

c Choose the correct word in italics to complete each sentence.

1 Anthony is going to stay with his *girlfriend / cousins* in Vancouver.

2 Anthony and his cousins are going to go *mountain climbing / trekking*.

3 He's going to *drive / fly* to Seattle.

4 Anthony's girlfriend *isn't / is* a teacher.

5 Anthony and his girlfriend are going to stay in Seattle for *two weeks / ten days*.

Dear Harry

We're having a fantastic holiday. Our hotel is near the (1) _____ – it's just a few hundred metres to the sea. There are lots of activities here. Last Wednesday we went (2) _____ on the river. It was scary but very exciting! The river is at the bottom of a huge (3) _____.

On Friday we went to a small (4) _____. There was a nice beach so we sunbathed in the morning and in the afternoon we went (5) _____ on a beautiful old boat.
Tomorrow we're going (6) _____ in the hills. I'm a bit nervous about that!

Give my love to Mum and Dad.

Love

Daniela

Grammar | *going to*

3   **a** Complete the tapescript with the correct forms of *be going to*.

Belinda: So, what are you going to do this summer?

Anthony: Well, I haven't got my tickets yet, but I'm intending to go to Canada. I *'m going to* visit my cousins in Vancouver.

Belinda: Really? That sounds exciting.

Anthony: Yes. I've never been to Canada.

Belinda: People say it's beautiful. (1) _____ you _h___ travel around or stay in one place?

Anthony: Well, I think I (2) _____ fly to Vancouver and stay with my cousins first. Then they (3) _____ take me to Whistler in the mountains.

Belinda: Mountain climbing?

Anthony: No, we (4) _____ go trekking. We (5) _____ spend three weeks trekking around the Rocky Mountains. Then I (6) _____ drive down to the American border. I want to see Seattle.

Belinda: (7) _____ your girlfriend _____ travel with you?

Anthony: Well, she isn't a teacher like me, so she can only take two weeks' holiday. She (8) _____ join me in Seattle. We (9) _____ stay there for ten days and then we're going to fly back together at the beginning of September.

Belinda: You're lucky. It sounds wonderful!

b Listen again and check your answers.

4 Rewrite the sentences using *going to* and the expressions in brackets.

We stayed with our uncle last week. (visit our cousins / next month)
We're going to visit our cousins next month.

She didn't buy any pasta at the shops. (not cook lasagne / this evening)
She isn't going to cook lasagne this evening.

1 I started the course in June. (finish the course / September)

_____

_____

2 Did you write a letter to the travel agent? (no / I / send an email / tomorrow)

_____

_____

3 Last year they stayed with relatives in France. (this year / stay with friends / in Spain)

_____

_____

4 Henry went white-water rafting in Colorado last year. (sailing / in Canada / next year)

_____

_____

5 She didn't study Physics at secondary school. (not study Science / university)

_____

_____

6 I didn't do any homework last night. (but / study / this weekend)

_____

_____

Pronunciation

6 **a** `12.2` Listen and underline the stress on sentence 2.

1 I'm <u>go</u>ing to join a <u>gym</u>.
2 He's going to fly to Rome.

b Mark the stress on these sentences.

1 We're going to buy a car.
2 I'm going to see the doctor.
3 She's going to meet my parents.
4 They're going to stay at home.
5 He's going to be a painter.

c `12.3` Listen and check your answers.

Vocabulary | future time

7 Correct the mistakes in the underlined expressions.

I'm going to finish the course <s>summer next</s>.
next summer

1 He's going to take his driving test <u>this later year</u>. _____

2 What are you going to do <u>week next</u>? _____

3 Is she going to visit him <u>tommorrow</u>? _____

4 We're going to take the children to Disneyland <u>the next week after</u>. _____

5 <u>In years' three time</u> I'm going to be a doctor! _____

6 Are you going to have a holiday <u>year next</u>? _____

7 They're going to open the new tunnel <u>years four now from</u>. _____

5 The people in the pictures are thinking about their intentions. What are they thinking? Write a sentence for each picture.

We're going to buy a dishwasher.

_____ _____

_____ _____ _____

_____ _____ _____

_____ _____ _____

12.2

Vocabulary | leisure activities

1 **a** Add letters from the box to each column in the table to make words. You can use each letter more than once.

> N G R I O E

1 (add 3 letters)		2 (add 3 letters)		3 (add 2 letters)	
act...	_ _ _	sess...	_ _ _	produc...	_ _
sing...		elect...		football...	
danc...		competit...		perform...	
train...					

b Match these descriptions to the columns 1–3.

people ☐   activities ☐   events ☐

Reading

2 **a** Read the text quickly and tick (✓) the correct answer. The text is:

a an informal letter to a friend who is a web designer. ☐

b a formal application for a job as a web designer. ☐

c an informal letter to a friend who lives abroad. ☐

A Dear Richard

B Things are fine here in Milan. My job isn't very interesting but I've got a lot of exciting plans. You know I want to be a web designer. Well, I'm going to start a part-time computing course to learn all about web design! It's at the local college, two evenings a week for three months. We're going to study a programme called 'Dreamweaver'. You can use it to make fantastic websites. Do you remember my friend Ruggiero? Well, we've got a great plan. One day we're going to start our own web design company! It's very exciting.

C Give my love to your parents. Please write again soon and tell me all about your new colleagues!

D Thanks for your last letter. Congratulations on your new job in Boston — it's a great place for a young architect! It was really interesting to hear all about your new office. I'm sorry you only get two weeks' holiday, but I know that's quite usual in the United States.

E Love

Simonetta

b Paragraphs B, C and D are in the wrong order. Put them in the correct order.

1 ☐   2 ☐   3 ☐

c Read the text and write short answers to the questions.

What has Richard got?
a new job

1 What is Richard's job?

2 Where does Richard work?

3 Why is Simonetta sorry?

4 What is usual in the United States?

5 Where does Simonetta live?

6 Is Simonetta's job interesting?

7 What is Simonetta's ambition?

8 Why is she starting a part-time course?

9 Why do people use 'Dreamweaver'?

10 What is Ruggiero and Simonetta's plan?

Grammar | infinitive of purpose

3 Match actions to purposes in the table. Use the information to write sentences.

ACTION		PURPOSE	
1	I'm going to start a part-time computing course	a	get fit
		b	visit our grandparents
2	You can use a computer	c	send emails
3	She's joining a gym	d	lose weight
4	Mike uses his bicycle	e	learn all about web design
5	We went to Warsaw		
6	I'm going on a diet	f	get a better job
7	I'm going to improve my English	g	commute to work

1 *I'm going to start a part-time computing course to learn all about web design.*

2 _____

3 _____

4 _____

5 _____

6 _____

7 _____

4 Put the words in the correct order to make sentences.

sunbathe   the beach   I   to   go to
I go to the beach to sunbathe.

1 Jane   to   her boyfriend   Berlin   flew   to visit

_____

2 to play   My son   his computer   uses   games

My son to play computer

3 an MP3 player   to listen to   I'm   going get   to   music

_____

4 We   food   always   to buy   to the market   go   fresh

_____

5 to see   My brother   the Hermitage Museum to   went   St Petersburg

_____

How to ... | organise an informal letter

5 **a** Look at Ex. 2. Copy the sentences Simonetta uses to:

mention the last letter she received
Thanks for your last letter.

1 make a positive comment about it

_____

2 describe her feelings about Richard's holidays

_____

3 say something general about her life

_____

4 make a request to end her letter

_____

b In informal letters we often use contracted forms, modifiers and adjectives. Find two more examples of each of these in Simonetta's letter.

1 contracted forms: *isn't* _____ _____

2 modifiers: *very* _____ _____

3 adjectives: *interesting* _____ _____

Writing

6 **a** You are going to write a letter to a close friend. Before you start, study this information.

YOUR FRIEND	YOU
Her name is Isabel. She is Australian.	Last week you started a new job.
Last month she moved to a new house in Sydney.	You are going to start a class at the sports centre next month.
She is going to visit you in your country next summer.	You are going to buy a new mobile phone tomorrow.

b Now plan your letter to Isabel. Use these notes.

First paragraph

• Thank Isabel for her last letter.
• Describe your feelings about her news.

Second paragraph

• Tell Isabel about your new job.
• Describe your plans for the future.

Third paragraph

• Ask her to write soon and make a request.

c Write the letter. Follow this advice:

• Use your imagination to make it interesting.
• Remember to use contracted forms, modifiers and adjectives.
• Write about 150 words.
• Use Simonetta's letter as a model.
• When you finish, check your letter for grammar and spelling mistakes. Correct any mistakes.

Listening

1 **a** 🔊 12.4 Cover the tapescript. Listen to a discussion between four friends. Tick (✓) the four ambitions they talk about.

be an accountant ☐	go around the world ☐
become a politician ☐	win a lot of money ☐
be a rock singer ☐	be a businesswoman ☐

b Listen again and complete the sentences with the ambitions.

1 Alex would like to *win a lot of money and retire*.

2 Matt would like to _____.

3 Dee would like to _____.

4 Jamie would like to _____.

Grammar | verbs + infinitive/-ing form

2 Complete the summary. Then listen again and check, or check your answers with the tapescript.

Alex wants *to do* something different. She'd like (1) _____ a lot of money and retire, but she can't stand (2) _____ all day.
Matt would like (3) _____ around the world, but he hates (4) _____.
Dee would like (5) _____ a politician and change the world.
Jamie wouldn't like (6) _____ a politician because everyone hates them. He's always wanted (7) _____ a rock singer – he loves (8) _____ the guitar and he enjoys (9) _____.

EXERCISES 1 AND 2 TAPESCRIPT

Jamie: What's wrong, Alex? You look bored today.

Alex: I am, well, I'm not bored right now, but I'm really bored with my job. It's the same thing every day. I really want to do something different.

Jamie: Like what? Find another job?

Alex: Well, I don't know. I suppose I'd like to win a lot of money and retire!

Dee: Come on, Alex, I know you. You can't stand doing nothing. You love being busy.

Alex: Mmm, maybe ... but you have to think about escaping sometimes.

Matt: Yes, that's right. I would like to fly around the world and see lots of interesting places.

Dee: You, Matt, but you hate flying. You're not going to get on a long-haul flight!

Matt: I hate flying but I love going to new places. Anyway, don't you ever want to change your life, Dee?

Dee: Me, yes, of course. I'd like to become a politician and change the world.

Jamie: I wouldn't like that. Everyone hates politicians. Anyway, you're a businesswoman so you already have that kind of life.

Dee: I don't think so ...

Jamie: You know what I've always wanted to be?

Matt: No?

Jamie: A rock singer.

Alex: Really? But you play the guitar, Jamie ...

Jamie: I know, and I love playing the guitar. But I enjoy singing, too and I'm having singing lessons at the moment.

Matt: I didn't know that.

Jamie: Mmm, and I've joined a new rock band – we play in clubs at the weekend now, and people like us.

Dee: So what about your job?

Jamie: My job as an accountant? I'm going to do it for another year or so, but the band is making a CD later this year, so ...

Dee: Wow, Jamie! You're going to be famous!

3 **a** There are six more grammatical mistakes in Davina's letter. Underline and number them.

As you know, I left my job last month. I worked in an office and (1) <u>I really hated be</u> inside all the time. Now I have to find another job. I wouldn't like working in an office again, so I'm thinking about some more training. I really enjoy to do water sports and I would like to becoming a water sports teacher. It's a good job here as there are a lot of tourists in the summer and most of them like learn waterskiing or windsurfing. I've had an interview to train as a teacher, but there's a problem. Part of the exam is written and I can't stand to take written exams – I always do them very badly. I really want start this training in March, then I can start teaching in the summer. Can you suggest any ways of helping me study for the exam?

b Write the correct sentences.

I really hated being inside.

1 _____

2 _____

3 _____

4 _____

5 _____

6 _____

4 What do the people want to do with their lives? Why? Write sentences like the example, using the pictures and words from the box.

1 Large garden

2 Racing driver

3 Good music system

4 teacher

5 Holiday rep

6 Lots of grandchildren

> drive fast   be with children   listen to music
> visit different countries   ~~work in the garden~~
> help young people

1 *He would like to have a large garden because he enjoys working in the garden.*

2 _____
_____

3 _____
_____

4 _____
_____

5 _____
_____

6 _____
_____

Pronunciation

5 **a** **12.5** Listen to the words below and make seven pairs. The main difference between the words in each pair is the vowel sound (/eɪ/ or /aɪ/).

> train bake die try I'm main late bike
> height day hate aim light mine

b Write the words in the correct column.

A /eɪ/	B /aɪ/
train	*try*

c Listen again and check your answers.

Writing

6 **a** Make notes about your ambitions for the future in these four areas.

- work and study
- marriage and children
- travel and holidays
- sport / leisure activities

b Write a short text about your ambitions for the future. Say why you want to do these things. Use the example to help you.

> I really enjoy watching films so I would like to do an evening course in film history. One day I'd like to work in film or TV. I'm happy with my boyfriend but I don't want to have children because I don't really like being with young children — well, not at the moment anyway. I want to travel all around the world because I love seeing different places. I'd like to play sport all my life because I enjoy being active and keeping fit. I think I would also like to raise money for a charity one day.

Grammar
Present Perfect

1 Complete the questions and answers with *has, have, 's, 've, ever, been* or *went*. Use contracted forms if you can.

1 **A:** Have you _____ been to England?
  B: No, I _____ never been there.

2 **A:** _____ your father been on a long-haul flight?
  B: Yes, he _____ to Singapore last winter.

3 **A:** _____ you ever been to a rock concert?
  B: Yes, I _____.

4 **A:** Has your wife ever _____ to South America?
  B: Yes, she _____ been to Argentina and Chile.

5 **A:** _____ you been on an adventure holiday?
  B: Yes, we _____ been bungee jumping in France.

2 Write Present Perfect questions (?) or negative sentences (✗) from the prompts.

she / ever / see / an opera (?)
Has she ever seen an opera?
I / go to / a zoo (✗)
I haven't been to a zoo.

1 I / spend / a lot of money (✗)
  _____

2 you / take / the driving test (?)
  _____

3 she / write / any postcards (?)
  _____

4 I / see / that film (✗)
  _____

5 The students / do / their homework (✗)
  _____

6 you / ever / play / golf (?)
  _____

7 Lena / visit / her parents (?)
  _____

8 We / go / on holiday this year (✗)
  _____

9 Henry / buy / a newspaper today (✗)
  _____

10 you / have / lunch (?)
  _____

-ing form as noun

3 Tick (✓) the correct sentences and cross (✗) the incorrect sentences. Underline the mistakes and write the corrections.

I think waiting for a bus is boring. ✓
Cycle is popular in Amsterdam. ✗ *Cycling*

1 These days fly is very popular. ☐ _____
2 In London going to the cinema are expensive. ☐ _____
3 Swimming is very relaxing. ☐ _____
4 On the Internet pay by credit card is easy.
  ☐ _____
5 Sunbathing are bad for your skin.
  ☐ _____
6 I think skiing in the mountains is fantastic.
  ☐ _____

can/can't, have to/don't have to

4 Look at the example. Then rewrite the numbered sentences from the notice using *can, can't, have to* or *don't have to*.

Brindsley College

INFORMATION FOR STUDENTS

1 • Don't smoke in the college building.
2   (Smoking is possible in the garden)
3 • Don't bring food or drinks into the classrooms.
4   (It is possible to get coffee and tea in the college café.)
5 • Show an identity card when you come into the college.
6 • Don't use mobile phones during lessons.
7 • Using the computers in the library is possible in the evenings.
8   (It isn't necessary to pay to use the computers.)
9 • Bring a pen and some paper to lessons.
10   (But it isn't necessary to bring a dictionary.)

Don't park in the teachers' car park.
Students ... can't park in the teachers' car park.
Students ...

1 _____
2 _____
3 _____
4 _____
5 _____
6 _____
7 _____
8 _____
9 _____
10 _____

Present Continuous for future

5 Complete using the prompts in brackets and a form of the Present Continuous.

> Q *Is Steve arriving* tomorrow? (Steve arrive)
>
> A No. He *'s arriving* on Sunday. (arrive)

1 Q What _____ at the weekend? (you do)

A We _____ the children to the beach. (take)

2 Q _____ here on the bus? (Jane come)

A No. She _____ here. (drive)

3 Q When _____? (your friends leave)

A They _____ on Saturday. (go)

4 Q What _____ this evening? (you cook)

A I _____, I'm going to a restaurant. (not cook)

be going to for intentions

6 Complete with the prompts in brackets and a form of *be going to*.

Dear Hilary

Thanks for your last letter. Congratulations on your new job! Things are very busy for us at the moment. We moved into our new house last week. It's very old and there are a lot of things we want to do! We (1) _____ (build) a new kitchen because the old one is really small. My brother-in-law (2) _____ (do) the work because he's a builder. We (3) _____ (not buy) the equipment from the local shops – they are very expensive! Amanda (4) _____ (buy) all the equipment from the Internet! I think she (5) _____ (get) one of those huge American fridges! We both love cooking so we (6) _____ (have) a really good cooker, but Amanda (7) _____ (not get) a microwave because she hates microwaved food! We also want to do things in the garden. I (8) _____ (buy) lots of beautiful new plants.
How are things with you? What's your new job like? (9) *you stay* (you stay) there for a long time? Write to me and let me know your plans. (10) *visit* (you/visit) us soon?

Love
Erik

Verb + infinitive/-*ing* form

7 Choose the correct form in italics.

1 Clara hates *sunbathing/sunbathe* so she doesn't like *going/go* to the beach.

2 I *like/'d like* to go to China next summer.

3 Johan loves *play/playing* football and he would like *being/to be* a professional footballer.

4 We enjoy *gardening/to garden* so we *wouldn't/ not* like to live in an apartment.

5 I never go to classical concerts because I can't stand *listening/listen* to classical music.

6 We'd like *to come/coming* to your party next week but we're really busy.

7 I usually cook because my husband *doesn't/ wouldn't* like doing it.

8 They're studying English because they'd like *getting/to get* better jobs.

9 My girlfriend loves *going/go* to the cinema but she *doesn't/can't* stand watching TV.

Vocabulary

8 Find words from Units 10–12 to complete the gaps. (The first letter of each word is given.)

You don't have to study this subject, it is *optional*.

1 You have to do this subject, it is c_____.

2 A k_____ is a school for very young children.

3 A t_____ is a university teacher.

4 You have to pay to study at a p_____ school.

5 A d_____ is a university qualification.

6 Breaking the rules of the road is an o_____.

7 After you pass the driving test you get a driving l_____.

8 In many countries drivers have to wear a s_____ belt.

9 A c_____ is an organisation that helps people.

10 Africa isn't a country; it's a c_____.

9 Match words from each column to make word pairs.

1	activity	a	climbing
2	beauty	b	holiday
3	twin	c	learning
4	distance	d	room
5	mountain	e	lights
6	primary	f	pool
7	swimming	g	salon
8	traffic	h	school

Jobs

Complete the descriptions.

1 A taxi driver *drives a taxi*.
2 An artist *draws or paints pictures*.
3 A bank clerk *works* _____ .
4 A teacher *teaches* _____ .
5 A journalist *writes* _____ .
6 A shop assistant _____ .
7 A nurse _____ .
8 An architect _____ .
9 A hairdresser _____ .
10 An unemployed person _____ .

Write more descriptions.

1 _____
2 _____
3 _____
4 _____
5 _____
6 _____
7 _____
8 _____
9 _____
10 _____

Personal possessions

Write the names of the possessions.

Adjectives

Complete sections 1–3 with the opposites of the adjectives. The opposites of section 1 are in the box. Then add adjectives of your choice to section 4, with an opposite if possible.

> bad big careless ~~horrible~~ interesting new
> old useless

	ADJECTIVE	OPPOSITE
1 General adjectives	nice	*horrible*
	old	new
	useful	useless
	boring	
	good	bad
	careful	
	small	
	young	
2 Places	hot	
	quiet	
	safe	
	friendly	
	unpopular	
3 People	healthy	
	happy	
	fat	
	dark	
	ugly	
	middle-aged	
	tanned	
	short	
4 Others		

Food and drink

Complete the word maps with more food and drink.

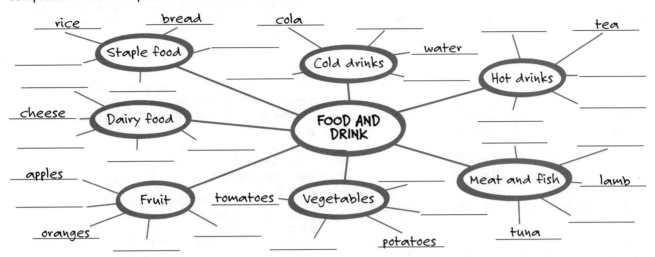

rice   bread   cola   tea

Staple food   Cold drinks   water   Hot drinks

cheese   Dairy food   FOOD AND DRINK   Meat and fish   lamb

apples   Fruit   tomatoes   Vegetables

oranges   potatoes   tuna

Sports and activities

Write the verbs and activities in the chart, then add more verbs and activities of your choice.

Verbs: do, go, play

Activities: aerobics, football, for a walk, swimming, tennis, judo, running, to the gym, skiing, yoga, cycling, basketball

VERB	ACTIVITY	
do	_aerobics_	_____
	_____	_____
	_____	_____
play	_football_	_____
	_____	_____
	_____	_____
go	_for a walk_	_____
	swimming	_____
	_____	_____
	_____	_____

Landscapes

Match the adjectives and landscapes to make phrases. Then add more of your choice.

Adjectives

green   popular
high   busy
dry   wide

a green forest

_____
_____
_____

Landscapes

mountain   beach
desert   river
city   forest

a high mountain

_____
_____
_____

Places in a town

Write the names of the places in a town.

1 _____   10 _____

2 _____   11 _____

3 _____   12 _____

4 _____   13 _____

5 _____   14 _____

6 _____   15 _____

7 _____   16 _____

8 _____   17 _____

9 _____

Transport

Write the names of forms of transport in the chart when you learn them.

LAND	SEA	AIR
car	_ship_	_____
_____	_____	_____
_____	_____	_____
_____	_____	_____

Key

Unit 1

Lesson 1

1 a
AUSTRALIA BRITAIN RUSSIA SPAIN ITALY FINLAND
The letter in the centre is I.

b

Across	Down
6 AUSTRALIAN	**1** BRAZILIAN
7 AMERICAN	**2** RUSSIAN
10 GREEK	**3** CHINESE
11 FINNISH	**4** JAPANESE
12 POLISH	**5** SPANISH
	8 ITALIAN
	9 BRITISH

2 **2** d C **3** a B **4** c A

3 **1** are, from, American **2** is, He's, Spain **3** Where, She's, British

4 **1** is he from **2** are they from **3** is it **4** is she **5** are they **6** are you from **7** is he **8** are they **9** is she from

5 **1** we are **2** I am **3** he is **4** they are **5** you are **6** it is

6 **1** ~~of~~ from **2** ~~is~~ are **3** ~~be~~ are **4** ~~am~~ is **5** ~~are~~ is

7 **1** R<u>u</u>ssian **2** G<u>er</u>man **3** Japan<u>ese</u> **4** A<u>mer</u>ican **5** Chi<u>nese</u> **6** B<u>ri</u>tish

8 a **2** Misha **3** Claudio **4** John and Liz **5** Elda **6** Jean Pierre

b **2** ~~Russian~~ Polish **3** ~~American~~ Italian **4** ~~Manchester~~ London **5** ~~Argentinian~~ Brazilian **6** ~~French~~ Canadian

Lesson 2

1 a **2** Robert **3** Ally **4** Geoffrey

b **1** sister **2** Geoffrey's/Ally's **3** Robert's **4** husband **5** niece **6** children **7** nephew **8** Debra's **9** Frank **10** Raymond

2 **1** Stefan is Ana's brother. **2** Giorgio and Sophia are Mario's parents. **3** Clara is Mr and Mrs Moreno's daughter. **4** Vanessa is Dieter's sister. **5** Alejandro and Elena are Manu's children. **6** Victor and Serge are Halyna's sons. **7** Stephanie is Pierre's niece.

3 **1** <u>u</u>ncle **2** h<u>u</u>sband **3** c<u>ou</u>sin **4** grand<u>so</u>n **5** R<u>u</u>ssia **6** nightcl<u>u</u>b **7** c<u>ou</u>ntry

4 a **1** B **2** C **3** A **4** D

b **1** their **2** their **3** his **4** her

5 **1** his **2** her **3** my **4** our **5** your

6 **1** d **2** e **3** f **4** a **5** b **6** c

7 **1** Yes, she is. **2** They're from Greece. **3** His name's John. **4** No, he isn't. He's Australian. **5** They're from the United States. **6** Their house is in Sydney. **7** Yes, she is.

Lesson 3

1 **2** taxi driver **3** artist **4** nurse **5** bank clerk **6** dentist **7** accountant **8** traffic warden **9** engineer **10** teacher

2 **1** an nurse = a nurse **2** a retired = retired **3** engineer = an engineer **4** a unemployed = unemployed **5** lawyer = a lawyer **6** an clerk = a clerk

3 a **1** Luis Figo is a Portuguese footballer. **2** Kylie Minogue is an Australian pop star. **3** Orlando Bloom is an English actor. **4** Roger Federer is a Swiss tennis player.

b Students' own answers.

4 a **1** My address isn't 20, Cedar Drive. **2** My grandparents aren't retired. **3** My little sister isn't beautiful.

4 Esther isn't from Colombia. **5** My nephew isn't a doctor. **6** My parents aren't Canadian.

b **1** My address is 20, Cedar Drive. **2** My grandparents are retired. **3** My little sister is beautiful. **4** Esther is from Colombia. **5** My nephew is a doctor. **6** My parents are Canadian.

5 a **1** old **2** from **3** manager **4** married **5** email **6** phone **7** mobile

b **1** henschel = Henschel **2** dortmund = Dortmund **3** germany = Germany **4** german = German **5** dilkestrasse = Dilkestrasse **6** dortmund = Dortmund

6 a
Perfect Partners on the Net
1 First name: Rainer
2 Surname: Henschel
3 Age: 24
4 Place of origin: Dortmund, Germany
5 Nationality: German
6 Married ☐ Single ✓
7 Address: 11, Dilkestrasse, Dortmund
8 Email address: r.henschel513@freepost.de
9 Home telephone number: 5307 895331
10 Mobile telephone number: 07632 116789
11 Occupation: manager of a bookshop
12 Qualifications: degree in German

b Students' own answers.

Unit 2

Lesson 1

1 a **1** I wash. **2** I go to work at nine o'clock. **3** I check the hotel rooms and the swimming pool. **4** I have lunch in the hotel restaurant. **5** I have lunch at one o'clock. **6** I have dinner with my family. **7** I go to bed at half-past eleven.

b **1** No, I don't. **2** Yes, I am. **3** Yes, I do. **4** Yes, I do. **5** No, I don't. **6** Yes, I am. **7** No, I don't.

c Students' own answers.

2 a **a** have breakfast **b** talk to my secretary **c** have coffee **d** watch the news on TV

b **1** a ✓ b ✗ **2** a ✓ b ✗ **3** a ✗ b ✓ **4** a ✓ b ✗ **5** a ✗ b ✓ **6** a ✓ b ✗

3 **1** e **2** c **3** b **4** f **5** a **6** d

4 **1** Do you live in New York? No, I don't. **2** Do we have a French dictionary? No, we don't. **3** Do you work in an office? No, I don't. **4** Do you like package holidays? Yes, I do. **5** Do we have her phone number? Yes, we do.

5 **1** Where do you work? **2** Are you a doctor? **3** When do you go to work? **4** Do you have lunch in the hospital? **5** When do you leave work? **6** What do you do in the evening?

6 **1** When do you get up? We get up at quarter past eight. **2** When do we have lunch? We have lunch at half past one. **3** When do you leave the office? I leave the office at six o'clock. **4** When do we have dinner? We have dinner at quarter to eight.

Lesson 2

1 a **1** watch **2** leave **3** go **4** meet **5** feed **6** work **7** get **8** make **9** read **10** wash

b **B** read a newspaper **C** feed the children **D** make dinner **E** go to bed **F** leave home

2 a **1** gets **2** feeds **3** leaves **4** gets **5** meets **6** washes **7** watches **8** leaves **9** makes **10** reads **11** goes

b **a** 3 **b** 5 **c** 4 **d** 4 **e** 6 **f** 2

3

JULIAN'S DAY	
7.15	Julian/He has breakfast.
7.45	He leaves home.
8.30	He starts work.
12.30	He has lunch.
4.30	He finishes work.
6.00	He has dinner.
11.00	He goes to bed.

4

/s/ STARTS	/z/ OPENS	/ɪz/ FINISHES
works	sells	washes
likes	plays	watches
talks	goes	

5 a 1 Where does Julian work? **2** What time does the shop open? **3** Does he sell cameras? **4** Does he like his job? **5** What does he do after work? **6** What does he do at 6.00? **7** Does he listen to CDs in the evening? **8** What time does he go to bed?

b 1 He works in a big electrical shop. **2** It opens at half past eight. **3** No, he doesn't. He sells TVs, videos and DVDs. **4** Yes, he does. **5** He usually plays football with friends. **6** He has dinner at six o'clock. **7** No, he doesn't. He watches TV in the evening. **8** He goes to bed at eleven o'clock.

6 In the morning, Sharon is a secretary in a lawyer's office. She gets up at half past seven and has breakfast. She walks to work at half past eight and opens the office at nine o'clock. She organises the lawyer's day and makes phone calls. In the afternoon, Sharon is a Spanish student. She goes to a Spanish class at two o'clock. She leaves the school at five o'clock and then has dinner at half past six. In the evening, she does her homework and watches TV. She goes to bed at quarter past eleven.

Lesson 3

1 a 1 bag, green, newspaper, red, diary, yellow, wallet, television
2 useful, lamp, pictures, scissors, shoe, exciting, gold, dish, horrible
3 taxi, interesting, grey, young, good, disc, careful, laptop

b

OBJECTS	COLOUR ADJECTIVES	OTHER ADJECTIVES
newspaper	red	exciting
diary	yellow	horrible
wallet	gold	interesting
television	grey	young
lamp		good
pictures		careful
scissors		
shoe		
dish		
taxi		
disc		
laptop		

c 1 newspaper **2** pictures **3** disc **4** taxi **5** television **6** lamp **7** diary

2 a 1 C **2** A **3** B **4** D

b 1 It's a book. **2** It's a lamp. **3** They're shoes. **4** They're magazines.

3 a 1 What's that? **2** what are these? **3** what are those? **4** What's this?

4 a and b this (/ɪ/): printer, think, discs, dishes, pink, picture these (/iː/): niece, green

5 a

	SINGULAR	PLURAL
1	address	addresses
2	car	cars
3	diary	diaries
4	family	families
5	foot	feet
6	half	halves
7	mouse	mice
8	wife	wives
9	scarf	scarves
10	sheep	sheep
11	suitcase	suitcases
12	tomato	tomatoes

b 1 have, feet **2** want, cars **3** like, scarves **4** are, families **5** addresses **6** use, diaries **7** eat, tomatoes

Unit 3

Lesson 1

1 1 goes **2** goes **3** doesn't go **4** likes **5** doesn't like **6** goes **7** goes **8** doesn't go

2 1 doesn't watch **2** doesn't listen to **3** don't want to **4** doesn't speak **5** don't relax

3 1 She doesn't play tennis at the sports centre. She plays tennis in the park. **2** She doesn't meet her friends at the gym. She meets her friends/them at the shops. **3** She doesn't watch films at home in the evening. She watches films/them at the cinema. **4** She doesn't swim at the beach. She swims at the swimming pool. **5** She doesn't relax at a club on Sundays. She relaxes at home.

4 a

```
          M
          O
      T F N
  S A T U R D A Y
  U   H E I A
  N   U S D Y
  D   R D A
  A   S A Y
  Y   D Y
      A
      Y
```

Wednesday is not in the puzzle.

b 1 Tuesday **2** Thursday **3** Sunday **4** Wednesday **5** Friday **6** Sunday **7** Friday **8** Thursday

5 a

Monday 4	Thursday 7
swim in sea / swimming pool	stay at home
Tuesday 5	**Friday 8**
go to gym / dance class	play tennis / football
Wednesday 6	**Saturday 9 / Sunday 10**
ride bike	go skiing

b My name's Alana. I live in the south of France. I'm very relaxed. On Mondays, I watch TV or a video. On Tuesdays, I listen to music and read (books). On Wednesdays, I meet friends in a café. On Thursdays, I go for a walk. On Fridays, I play computer games with Jan and at the weekend/on Saturdays and Sundays, I relax at home or sunbathe on the beach.

Lesson 2

1 **a** 1 I 2 B 3 G 4 D 5 C 6 H 7 J 8 A 9 C 10 E

b A go sailing B go swimming C do yoga D go skateboarding E play tennis F go running G ride a bike H dance I play football

2 **a** 1 riding my bike 2 dance 3 football 4 computer games 5 yoga

b 1 go riding = ride 2 play aerobics = do aerobics 3 swimming = go swimming/swim 4 does computer games = plays computer games 5 go judo = do judo

3 **a** 3

b 2 a 3 d 4 e 5 g 6 f 7 b

4 2 Julia and Eric Roberts can both act. 3 The Neville brothers can both play football. 4 Kingsley and Martin Amis can both write books. 5 The Coen brothers can both make good films. 6 Marat and Dinara Safin can both play tennis. 7 Michael and Janet Jackson can both sing.

5 **a** 1 can 2 can 3 can 4 can 5 can 6 can't 7 can 8 can't 9 can She can organize games for sixty children.

b She can ride a bike and play tennis. She can teach aerobics but she can't teach judo. She can speak German and Spanish but she can't speak French. She can drive.

6 b

	/ə/	/æ/	/ɑː/
3 I can sing.	✓		
4 ... but I can draw.		✓	
5 I can play tennis.	✓		
6 ... I can teach aerobics.	✓		
7 No, I can't.			✓
8 I can speak German ...	✓		
9 I can't speak French.			✓
10 Yes, I can.		✓	

Lesson 3

1 **a** 2 3 1

b

1
Caller: *Lucy*
Phone number: 094048832
Message: _call her after 2.20 this afternoon_
2
Caller: *Fiona*
Phone number: 0991344562
Message: _She can't see you tomorrow. _How about_ 7.10 on Friday?
3
Caller: *Dr Gupta*
Phone number: 8947701
Message: Please call him after 4.30.

2 **a** 1 speak 2 take 3 ask 4 What's 5 can

3 there here, make take; speak, ask; what are what's; I am It is

4 **a and b** 1 2001 – two thousand and one 2 175,000,000 – one hundred and seventy five million 3 20,000 – twenty thousand 4 8,760 – eight thousand seven hundred and sixty 5 1,285,000,000 – one billion, two hundred and eighty five million

5 **a** 1 fourteen 2 forty 3 fifteen 4 fifty 5 eighty 6 eighteen

b 1 b✓ 2 a✓ 3 a✓ 4 b✓ 5 a✓

6 1 Can you ask Anna to call me after 6.30? 2 Can you meet me at the hospital at 7.15? 3 Can you ask Simon to

phone Mum and Dad at the weekend? 4 Can you come to the shop on Tuesday after 5.00? 5 Can you take the children to school tomorrow?

7 **a** a about b How c can d don't e Let's f Why

b Order of sentences: 7, 4, 2, 1, 3, 6, 8, 5

Review and consolidation 1

1 **a** 2 are 3 is 4 is 5 Are 6 Is 7 Is 8 Are 9 is 10 are; a isn't b am c is d is e is f aren't g are h is i am j is

b 2 i 3 c 4 e 5 b 6 d 7 a 8 f 9 h 10 g

2 1 his 2 her 3 your 4 their 5 Antonio's 6 my 7 his 8 our 9 William's 10 our

3 1 works 2 doesn't take 3 get up 4 have 5 has 6 goes 7 washes 8 don't go 9 doesn't live 10 don't like

4 1 Does William leave home at eight o'clock? 2 When do you start work? 3 Where do your parents go on holiday? 4 Do you work in an office? 5 Does she have a fax machine? 6 What time does he get home? 7 When does Emily feed her children? 8 Do you like nightclubs? 9 Do they go to the beach at the weekend? 10 Where do you work?

5 these; that; this; those

6 add -s: pictures; add -es: watches; remove -f, add -ves: knives, scarves; remove -y, add -ies: cities, diaries; irregular: children, people

7 1 Can you sing? Yes, I can. 2 Can your husband cook? No, he can't 3 Can she speak Spanish and Portuguese? Yes, she can. 4 Can you do judo? Yes, I can. 5 Can a DVD player send emails? No, it can't.

8 **a** 2 daughters, family; 3 do, verbs; 4 finish, verbs; 5 get up, verbs; 6 nurse, jobs; 7 play, verbs; 8 Sunday, days; 9 uncle, family; 10 wallet, possessions

b 1 nurse; 2 accountant; 3 uncle; 4 daughters; 5 wallet; 6 get up; 7 finish; 8 do; 9 play; 10 Sunday

9 2 j 3 h 4 i 5 d 6 e 7 b 8 a 9 g 10 f

Unit 4

Lesson 1

1 **a** 1 beef 2 bread 3 butter 4 cheese 5 coffee 6 cola 7 crisps 8 lamb 9 milk 10 orange juice 11 pasta 12 pineapples 13 eggs 14 watermelons

b

	MEAT	FRUIT	DRINKS	DAIRY	OTHER
countable		apples pineapples watermelons			
uncountable	beef lamb		coffee cola milk* orange juice	butter cheese milk*	bread crisps pasta tuna

* *milk* can go in two positions.

2 1 bananas 2 tuna 3 carrots 4 chicken

3 1 are is 2 a 3 rices rice 4 meats meat 5 are is 6 butters butter 7 a 8 tunas tuna 9 are is

4 1 How much rice do you buy at the supermarket? 2 How much water do you drink every day? 3 How many oranges do you buy at the market? 4 How many bananas does your family eat every week? 5 How much coffee do you drink at the weekend?
Students' own answers to the questions

5 1 twenty-five kilos 2 six hundred and thirty grammes 3 seven hundred and nineteen grammes 4 four and a half litres (or four point five litres)

6 **a** 1 h 2 d 3 e 4 a 5 g 6 c 7 b 8 f

b 1 A ✗ B ✓ C ✓ D ✓ 2 A ✓ B ✓ C ✗ D ✓

7 1 How much coffee does Julia buy? 2 How many oranges does Julia buy? 3 How much rice … ? She buys 4 How many … does Julia buy? She buys 12. 5 How much … does Julia buy? She buys 1.5 kg. 6 How many bananas does she buy? She buys … 7 How many apples does she buy? She buys …

Lesson 2

1 **a** 1 bottle 2 box 3 carton 4 packet 5 bag

b A box B carton D bottle D packet E can F bag

c 1 bag 2 bottle 3 box 4 can 5 carton 6 packet

2 2 a papaya 3 some pasta 4 a tomato 5 some water 6 some tuna 7 some butter 8 some cheese 9 some salad

3 1 some mineral water 2 any fruit juice 3 some cheese 4 any potatoes 5 some chocolates 6 any money 7 any cash 8 a credit card 9 a biscuit 10 any biscuits

4 **a and b**

A /æ/ (pasta)	B /ʌ/ (some)
business**man**	**hun**gry
carrot	**mon**ey
grandparents	night**club**
laptop	sun**bathe**
package	**Sun**day
programme	un**em**ployed

5 2 a 3 f 4 h 5 c 6 e 7 b 8 g

6 1 Amanda 2 Jane (Amanda's daughter) 3 17 4 She goes to nightclubs. 5 tired 6 It isn't healthy./She eats a lot of burgers and pizzas. 7 She doesn't want to go to school. 8 No, she doesn't.

7 Dear Laurence
I have a problem with my daughter, Jane. She's only 17 but she hates school and doesn't do any homework. Also, she goes out to nightclubs every evening and she feels tired in the morning. Her diet is also very bad. I give her healthy food at home but she eats a lot of convenience food like burgers and pizzas.
What can I do? Please help me.
Amanda

Lesson 3

1 **a** 1 Yes, she does. 2 Yes, she does. 3 She pays by credit card.

b
1 large tuna and pineapple pizza	€8.50
1 small tomato salad	€2.45
1 small cup of coffee	€2.00
Total	€12.95

c 1 €8.50 2 €8.95 3 €2.45 4 €2.00 5 €2.75

2 **a** 1 How much is a large tuna and pineapple pizza? 2 How much is a large tomato salad/small tuna salad? 3 How much is a small beef and mushroom pizza?

b 1 f 2 c 3 d 4 b 5 a 6 e

3 **a** 1 her 2 them 3 him 4 us

b 1 them, No, they are for me. 2 him, No, they are for us. 3 us, No, it is for her. 4 her, No, it is for him. 5 them, No, it is for her.

4 1 He loves her. 2 We don't like it. 3 They help us with

it. 4 They visit them every Saturday afternoon. 5 We play football with him. 6 She uses it every day. 7 Do you want to have lunch with us?

5 1 like 2 much 3 Do 4 want 5 drink 6 I'd 7 is 8 by

6 **b** 1 I'd like a large cheeseburger [↗], a small cup of coffee [↗] and a small salad [↘]. 2 I'd like a small vegetarian pizza [↗], large fries [↗] and an orange juice [↘]. 3 I'd like a kilo of oranges [↗], an apple [↗], two bananas [↗] and a melon [↘]. 4 I'd like 500g of beef [↗], a packet of biscuits [↗], 200g of sugar [↗] and a bottle of mineral water [↘].

Unit 5

Lesson 1

1 **a** 2

b Students should tick 1, 2, 5, 6 and 8.

c 1 F 2 T 3 T 4 T 5 T 6 F 7 F

2 **a** 1 bath 2 bed 3 CD player 4 chair 5 cooker 6 cupboard 7 desk 8 dishwasher 9 DVD player 10 fridge 11 microwave 12 sofa 13 shower 14 table 15 television 16 toilet

b
Living room: CD player, chair, cupboard*, desk, DVD player, sofa, table*, television; Bedroom: bed, cupboard*, Bathroom: bath, shower, toilet; Kitchen: cooker, cupboard*, dishwasher, fridge, microwave, table*
* These often go in more than one room.

3 1 There are 2 Are there 3 There's 4 There isn't 5 Is there 6 There isn't 7 There aren't 8 There's 9 Is there

4 **a** 1 There are two swimming pools. 2 There is a beach near the village. 3 There are two cafés. 4 There is a place to park your car. 5 You can play tennis here.

b 1 There's a hotel in the village. 2 There's a/one bar in the village. 3 There's a/one takeaway restaurant in the village. 4 There are three shops in the village. 5 There's a tennis court in the village. 6 There isn't a school in the village. 7 There isn't a bank in the village.

5 Students' own answers.

Lesson 2

1 **a** 3 d 4 a 5 f 6 b 7 e 8 g

b 1 cupboard 2 CD player 3 dining table 4 armchair 5 microwave

2 1 MP3 player 2 car 3 sofa 4 television 5 bed 6 fridge 7 laptop computer 8 dining chair 9 washing machine

3 1 I've got two brothers. 2 They've got a swimming pool. 3 Álvaro's got an MP3 player. 4 We've got a new sofa. 5 You've got a phone message. 6 I've got three children. 7 She's got a boyfriend in New York.

4 1 We haven't got a big kitchen. 2 Has your girlfriend got a good job? 3 She hasn't got a DVD player. 4 Have they got a microwave? 5 Have you got the answers? 6 He hasn't got a credit card.

5 1 Has your town got a shopping centre? Yes, it has. No, it hasn't. 2 Has your town got an airport? Yes, it has. No, it hasn't. 3 Have you got any children? Yes, I have. No, I haven't. 4 Have you got any brothers or sisters? Yes, I have. No, I haven't.

6 Students' own answers.

7 **a** B ✓

b 1 've/have got two 2 's/has got three 3 's/has got three 4 've/have got forty c **1** Yes, they have. **2** No, she hasn't. **3** Yes, he has. **4** Yes, it has. **5** No, they haven't. **6** Yes, they have.

8

	/ɒ/	/æ/
1 hospital	✓	
2 pocket	✓	
3 tap		✓
4 shop	✓	
5 packet		✓
6 hot	✓	

Lesson 3

1 a
Across: **1** cold **3** beautiful **5** green **6** huge **7** island **9** busy
Down: **1** city **2** lake **3** beach **4** forest **8** dry The adjective is cold.

b 1 green **2** friendly **3** dry **4** modern **5** wide **6** busy **7** green **8** dry

2 Students' own answers.

3 a 2 not very popular **3** very high **4** not very big **5** really famous **6** quite healthy

b 1 Traffic warden isn't a very popular job. **2** The Empire State is a very high building. **3** The Volkswagen Polo isn't a very big car. **4** Brad Pitt is a really famous actor. **5** Chicken and potatoes is a quite healthy meal/quite a healthy meal.

4 a John is from Scotland, in the north of Britain. He lives in Edinburgh, a large city in the south-east of the country. There are lots of interesting places in Edinburgh: museums, cinemas, theatres and restaurants. There's an arts festival every year and John always goes to it with his friends. The city is also quite near beautiful lakes and mountains.
John likes Edinburgh because it's a very friendly place. He also thinks the city is very beautiful, but he doesn't like the Scottish weather – it's very cold!

b

HOW TO ...	
say where someone lives	John is from Scotland. He lives in Edinburgh.
describe a country/ city	There are lots of interesting places ... There's an arts festival ... The city is quite near beautiful lakes and mountains.
give someone's opinion	John likes Edinburgh because ... He doesn't like the Scottish weather ...

5 Students' own answers.

6 a and b 3 com/fort/able **4** com/pare **5** de/cide **6** fam/ous **7** moun/tain **8** o/pin/ion **9** trop/ic/al **10** vill/age

c

WORDS WITH TWO SYLLABLES		WORDS WITH THREE SYLLABLES	
Stress on 1st syllable	Stress on 2nd syllable	Stress on 1st syllable	Stress on 2nd syllable
famous mountain village	compare decide	comfortable tropical	opinion

Unit 6

Lesson 1

1 1 hospital **2** apartment **3** (across) bar **3** (down) bank **4** factory **5** museum **6** supermarket **7** art gallery

2 1 There was a zoo in Lake Road. **2** There were shops in Lake Road. **3** There was a factory in Station Road. **4** There was a station in Station Road. **5** There was a cinema in Harley Street. **6** There was a hospital in Harley Street. **7** There were houses in the park.

3 1 Was there a factory in Station Road in 1990? Yes, there was. **2** What was there in Green Street in 1990? There were cottages (in Green Street in 1990). **3** Was there a nightclub in Harley Street in 1990? No, there wasn't. There was a cinema. **4** Were there apartments in Station Road in 1990? No, there weren't. There was a factory.

4 1 She performed at the concert hall last Friday evening. **2** She opened the new supermarket last Saturday morning. **3** She watched the video of the concert with Mike on Sunday afternoon. **4** She cleaned the house two days ago. **5** She played football with the boys yesterday.

5 a 1 walked **2** worked **3** played **4** cooked **5** helped **6** watched **7** relaxed

b Warren's day started at 6.30a.m. yesterday. He walked to the bus stop at 7.00 and waited for the bus from 7.15 to 7.30. He worked from 8.00 to 4.00. He repaired cars all day. Then he cooked dinner and he studied from 7.30 to 9.30. Then he listened to music.

6 4, 7, 1, 8, 2, 9, 6, 3, 5

7 a

/t/ WORKED	/d/ OPENED	/ɪd/ STARTED
cooked walked	stayed phoned listened called	wanted visited

Lesson 2

1 B orange juice **C** eggs **D** meat **E** pasta **F** biscuits **G** bread **H** salad **I** apples **J** potatoes

2 A Sam **B** Sean **C** Sarah **D** Stephanie **E** Simon **F** Sandy **G** Steve **H** Susan **I** Sally

3 a 3 Did you stay in a nice place? **4** What did you do? **5** Did you meet any friends? **6** How long did you stay? **7** When did you get home? **8** Did you buy me anything?

b 3, 7, 2, 5, 8, 4, 1, 6

4

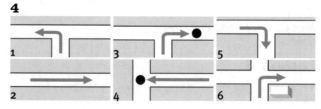

5 a 1 E **2** A **3** F **4** G

b 1 turn left, at the end of, right **2** you know, right into, on the left **3** on, turn right, on the right **4** tell me the way, straight, across, turn left

6 1 Go out of the station and turn left into Church Lane. The cinema is at the end of the road, on the right. **2** You go straight on and turn right into Hillfield Avenue. The supermarket is on the right. **3** Go out of the station and turn left into Church Lane. Then turn right into Stowe Place and left at the end of the road. The bank is on the left.

Lesson 3

1 a 2

b 4, 6, 1, 7, 5, 2, 3

c 1 There were 33 people on the journey: Lewis and Clark, 30 men and an Indian woman, Sacagawea. **2** The

Dakota Indians helped them find the Pacific Ocean.   **3** They measured everything for their maps.   **4** They discovered that North America was a huge place.

2   **1** William Shakespeare didn't write *Don Quixote*.   **2** My great-grandparents didn't own a car.   **3** Queen Elizabeth I wasn't married.   **4** We didn't have mobile phones in the 1970s.   **5** My father didn't go to university.   **6** He didn't study foreign languages at school.   **7** In ancient times people didn't eat a lot of food and they weren't tall.   **8** I didn't do my homework yesterday.

3   tram car taxi bicycle plane bus

4   **1** The *Titanic* and the *Lusitania* were famous ships.   **2** The TGV and the Talgo are fast trains.   **3** Yellow taxis are popular in New York.   **4** The railway was an invention of the nineteenth century.   **5** The *Santa Maria* was Columbus's ship.

5   **1** No, I like potatoes.   **2** No, I'm Canadian.   **3** No, she's thirsty.   **4** No, we arrived on Thursday.

6   **a, b and c**   Students' own answers.

Review and consolidation 2

1   Countable nouns: armchair, biscuit, coin, dishwasher, receipt; Uncountable nouns: bread, mayonnaise, money rice, salad

2   **1** some   **2** much   **3** any   **4** some   **5** many   **6** any   **7** a   **8** many   **9** a   **10** some

3   **1** me   **2** him   **3** them   **4** it   **5** you   **6** her   **7** me   **8** us   **9** them   **10** her

4   **1** is there   **2** there is   **3** Is there   **4** there is   **5** there are   **6** Is there   **7** there isn't   **8** Are there   **9** there aren't   **10** there isn't

5   **1** The new sports centre is very modern.   **2** This film is really boring.   **3** We are really late.   **4** My diet is really unhealthy.   **5** The kitchen is not very well-equipped.

6   **1** Have you got a microwave? No, I haven't.   **2** Has Sarah got a credit card? Yes, she has.   **3** Have your parents got a big garden? No, they haven't.   **4** Have we got any biscuits? No, we haven't.   **5** Has the dog got any food? Yes, he has.

7   **a**   **1** was/were   **2** decided   **3** married   **4** opened   **5** started   **6** stopped   **7** travelled   **8** visited   **9** wanted   **10** worked

b   **1** stopped   **2** didn't want   **3** worked   **4** decided   **5** travelled   **6** married   **7** weren't   **8** opened   **9** visited   **10** started

c   **1** He didn't study at university. He wanted to go to work.   **2** He didn't stay at the factory for ten years. He worked there for five years.   **3** He didn't marry a woman in Africa. He married a woman in India.   **4** The writer's parents didn't open an Indian factory. They opened an Indian restaurant.   **5** They didn't produce Indian food for schools. They produced Indian food for supermarkets.

8   **a**   Food and drink: banana, cola, lamb, potato; Rooms: bathroom, dining room, hall, kitchen; Furniture: bed, cupboard, desk, table; Places in a town: library, newsagent's, pharmacy, post office; Transport: bicycle, boat, motorbike, tram

b   **1** kitchen   **2** boat   **3** library   **4** bathroom   **5** desk   **6** lamb   **7** newsagent's   **8** cupboard

Unit 7

Lesson 1

1   **a**   **A** Jeremy   **B** Alvaro   **D** Clara   **E** Henry   **F** Melanie   **G** Dieter   **H** Stefan   **I** Amanda   **J** Surinda

b   **1** fair   **2** two   **3** three   **4** three   **5** bald

c   **1** glasses   **2** tanned   **3** short   **4** handsome   **5** dark   **6** beard   **7** slim/pretty   **8** friendly

2   **1** shy   **2** old   **3** ugly   **4** friendly/nice/fun/lovely/helpful   **5** unfriendly/horrible

3   Students' own answers.

4   **2** a   **3** j   **4** f   **5** i   **6** c   **7** b   **8** e   **9** g   **10** d

5   sports centre = 5   badminton = 6   shopping centre = 2   CDs = 3   salad = 4

6   **1** I like hot places but Sally likes cold ones.   **2** Can I have six large salads and two small ones, please?   **3** Do you want the British spelling or the American one?   **4** We've got three bedrooms – I sleep in the big one.   **5** Are they the blue chairs, the red ones or the yellow ones?   **6** The first flat's got a terrace and the second one's got a garden.   **7** I'd like four tuna sandwiches and a chicken one, please.

7   **a**   a Dear   b Love   **1** Jenna   **2** Florence   **3** sisters   **4** at university   **5** Toledo   **6** eight   **7** there are lots of dictionaries and some computers with language programs   **8** Give her love to Mum and Dad.

b   Students' own answers.

Lesson 2

1   **1** = C   **2** = E   **3** = D   **4** = A   **5** = B

2   **1** your   **2** their   **3** ours   **4** yours   **5** hers   **6** our   **7** my   **8** her   **9** theirs

3   **1** belongs to you   **2** is mine   **3** is theirs   **4** is ours   **5** doesn't belong to them   **6** isn't ours   **7** isn't your   **8** are ours   **9** aren't his

4   **1** theirs   **2** ours   **3** mine   **4** hers   **5** his   **6** yours

5   **a**   **2** third   **3** something

b   **1** b   **2** b   **3** a   **4** b   **5** a   **6** a

6   **1** 18th November   **2** June   **3** Wednesday   **4** Saturday   **5** 22nd July   **6** Sunday   **7** 24th August

7   **1** the twenty-fifth of December   **2** the twenty-third of April   **3** the seventeenth of March   **4** the twenty-sixth of December   **5** the twenty-second of April   **6** the nineteenth of October   **7** the third of September

8   **a**

	ORANGE JUICE	CUPS OF COFFEE	CHICKEN SANDWICH	TUNA SANDWICH	BURGERS	SALAD	BAG OF CRISPS
Phil	✓						✓
Ana				✓			
Dave and Joe		✓			✓		
Sylvia						✓	
Darren			✓				

b   **1** yours   **2** mine   **3** his   **4** mine   **5** yours   **6** hers   **7** theirs   **8** yours   **9** mine

Lesson 3

1   **2**

2   **2** d   **3** c   **4** f   **5** b   **6** a

3   **a**   5, 1, 6, 4, 2, 3

b   **1** No, he didn't.   **2** He tried to steal it./He broke into the car and took it.   **3** People on the street called them.   **4** No, it wasn't.   **5** A local business, to advertise a competition.

4 a

	INFINITIVE	PAST SIMPLE FORM	
		REGULAR	IRREGULAR
3	notice	noticed	
4	break		broke
5	take		took
6	see		saw
7	call	called	
8	arrive	arrived	
9	catch		caught
10	put		put
11	make		made
12	can		could

b 1 We caught the bus to work yesterday morning. 2 Don and Eva saw their grandchildren last Sunday. 3 Mum made fantastic chocolate biscuits for the party last weekend. 4 Xavier took hundreds of photos on his last holiday. 5 I could swim 500 metres in twenty minutes when I was a child. 6 Alicia put a lot of sugar in her coffee yesterday! 7 They weren't very happy about the weather on holiday! 8 The train arrived late yesterday morning.

5 a break into

b 1 look at 2 listen to 3 move in 4 picked up 5 looked after

6 a 1 /w/ 2 /w/ 3 /h/ 4 /w/ 5 /w/ 6 /h/ 7 /h/

b 1 How 2 Where 3 What 4 When 5 Who 6 Why
Students' own answers.

Unit 8

Lesson 1

1 1 clothes words: top, pullover
adjective: tight
2 clothes words: dress, shorts, shoes, scarf.
adjective: formal
3 clothes words: gloves, trousers, suit, tie.
adjective: smart

2

SUMMER	WINTER	FORMAL	INFORMAL
shorts	coat	suit	jeans
T-shirt	gloves	tie	trainers
	scarf		shorts
	pullover		T-shirt

3 2 a tight shirt 3 a formal suit 4 a light dress 5 loose trousers 6 a thick coat

4 1 I (always) wear a hat in winter. 2 The weather is (sometimes) hot in July. 3 We (never) eat at fast food restaurants. 4 I (hardly ever) use my microwave. 5 My kitchen is (often) untidy. 6 She (usually) gets money from the cashpoint. 7 Formal clothes are (often) uncomfortable.

5 1 I hardly ever wear a suit to work. 2 Mrs Gladstone is sometimes late. 3 We often visit my parents at the weekend. 4 They usually go to Greece in the summer. 5 I always phone my mother on Saturdays. 6 The manager is always busy. 7 James never gets up early on Sundays. 8 It hardly ever rains in Madrid in August.

6 1 Jason never smokes. 2 I hardly ever go to the theatre. 3 They always watch the TV news. 4 Jennifer sometimes wears a dress. 5 He usually gets up at seven o'clock.

7 a The answer is for letter B.

b 1 advice 2 wear 3 uncomfortable 4 can 5 Can you 6 usually 7 don't 8 smart 9 light 10 put

c 1 What does Malcolm wear to work? 2 How does Malcolm get to work? 3 Where does Sophia work? 4 When does Sophia help in the gym? 5 What do her colleagues say?

8 Possible answer: Dear Davina
Can you give me some advice? Next month I begin a job at SystemPro Incorporated and I don't know much about the company. Can you answer some questions? What kind of clothes can I wear? Can I make private phone calls and send emails? What about smoking – can I smoke in the office? And how long are the lunch breaks?
Thanks very much.

Lesson 2

1 a 2 b 8 c 6 d 7 e 3 f 10 g 1 h 9 i 5 j 4

2 a 6

b Ron Tyler [8] Leanne Tyler [10] Mikey Tyler [2] Big Dave [7] Tracey [1] Hayley [5]

c Students should tick 1, 2, 4, 6, 7, 10, 11 and 12

3 a 1 Leanne is looking at a magazine. She's laughing. 3 Mikey is meeting Tracey. He's eating a burger. 4 He's eating a sandwich and drinking a coffee. 5 She's looking at a magazine. (She's feeling unhappy.) 6 Ron is talking on his mobile. He's shouting. 7 Brian is talking on a mobile phone. 8 Big Dave is walking towards the police detective. 9 Hayley is waiting at the check-in desk. She's smoking. 10 She's waiting at the check-in desk.

b 1 Is Mikey wearing jeans? Yes, he is. 2 Is Mikey eating a sandwich? No, he isn't. He's eating a burger. 3 Is Hayley smoking? Yes, she is. 4 Is Big Dave wearing a coat? No, he isn't. He's wearing a jacket. 5 Is Leanne feeling unhappy? No, she isn't. She's laughing.

4 a

	ADJECTIVE	ADVERB
1	bad	badly
2	careless	carelessly
3	close	closely
4	comfortable	comfortably
5	good	well
6	happy	happily
7	hungry	hungrily
8	quick	quickly
9	sad	sadly
10	strange	strangely

b 1 ✓ 2 ~~sadly~~ = sad 3 ~~loud~~ = loudly 4 ~~good~~ = well 5 ~~strangely~~ = strange 6 ✓ 7 ~~quiet~~ = quietly

Lesson 3

1 a 1 wa + rm = warm 2 su + nny = sunny 3 win + dy = windy 4 sno + wing = snowing 5 co + ld = cold 6 rain + ing = raining 7 cloud + y = cloudy

b 1 cloudy 2 sunny, warm 3 cold, snowing 4 foggy 5 raining

2 a
/ɒ/ /ɒ/ /əʊ//ɒ/
2 I lost my watch in the post office. 3,1
/əʊ/ /əʊ/ /ɒ/ /ɒ//əʊ/
3 I need some new clothes to go to college in October. 2,3
/ɒ/ /ɒ/ /əʊ/ /əʊ/ /əʊ/
4 It's hot in Australia but it's snowing and cold in Poland. 2,3

3 a

	GOOD FOR US	BAD FOR US	GOOD AND BAD
The sun			✓
Hot weather		✓	
Cold weather			✓

b 1 F 2 F 3 T 4 T 5 F

4

	NOUNS	ADJECTIVES
1	health	healthy
2	importance	important
3	suntan	suntanned
4	depression	depressed
5	sickness	sick
6	darkness	dark

5 a and b 1 I think it looks horrible. 2 Don't you think so? 3 Oh, I agree that you need to be careful. 4 Well, no. I'm not sure.

6 Actions happening now: 2, 3, 6
Actions that happen regularly: 5, 7, 8

7 2 He sells men's clothes. 3 He plays computer games. 4 He eats a burger with (his) friends. 6 He's swimming in the sea. 7 He's eating fish at a restaurant. 8 He's playing football on the beach.

Unit 9

Lesson 1

1 a eight

b 1 broadsheets, tabloids 2 broadsheet 3 tabloid 4 It started in Manchester–most newspapers started in London.

2

	DATE STARTED	CIRCULATION	PRICE
The Daily Mail	1896	2,422,000	40p
The Daily Mirror	1903	2,220,000	35p
The Daily Telegraph	1855	975,000	60p
The Guardian	1821	325,000	55p
The Independent	1986	205,000	60p
The Sun	1964	3,452,000	30p
The Times	1785	680,000	50p

3 1 national 2 local 3 daily 4 international 5 lives

4 1 *The Sun* is cheaper than *The Times*. 2 *The Guardian* is more expensive than *The Daily Mail*. 3 *The Independent* is newer than *The Daily Express*. 4 *The Daily Telegraph* is more popular than *The Daily Express*. 5 *The Guardian* is older than *The Daily Mail*. 6 *The Daily Mirror* is cheaper than *The Independent*.

5 a tight – loose smart – casual handsome – ugly early – late easy – difficult tidy – untidy noisy – quiet hot – cold healthy – unhealthy

b 2 Ken is more handsome than Mike./Mike is uglier than Ken. 3 The living room is tidier than the bedroom./The bedroom is untidier than the living room. 4 Emma is noisier than Caroline./Caroline is quieter than Emma. 5 Harriet is smarter than Harry./Harry is more casual than Harriet. 6 Egypt is hotter than Greenland./Greenland is colder than Egypt.

6 a 1 My brother is younger than me. 2 Fruit juice is nicer than water. 3 Newspapers are more versatile than TV. 4 Canada is colder than Brazil.

Lesson 2

1 a

T	M	U	S	I	C	A	L	Y	D
A	G	S	C	I	E	N	C	E	F
R	D	T	Y	K	O	Q	H	W	I
D	F	V	A	B	J	X	O	S	C
C	O	M	E	D	Y	Z	R	G	T
W	C	M	L	N	T	U	R	O	I
E	D	C	A	R	T	O	O	N	O
F	T	X	E	T	S	U	R	N	N
L	O	V	E	S	T	O	R	Y	V
J	D	T	H	R	I	L	L	E	R

b 1 a love story 2 a horror film 3 a cartoon 4 an adventure film 5 a musical 6 a science fiction film 7 a thriller

2 1 the most best = the best 2 the bigger = the biggest 3 newest = the newest 4 the most cheap = the cheapest 5 the most atractivest = the most attractive

3 1 Jane is the tallest (girl). 2 Yvonne's baby is the youngest (baby). 3 Luis is the most intelligent (student). 4 Andreas is the heaviest (man). 5 Peter is the most romantic (boyfriend).

4 1 The youngest tennis champion is/was Martina Hingis. 2 The loudest rock band is/was The Who. 3 The noisiest plane is/was Concorde. 4 The driest desert is the Atacama Desert in Chile. 5 The fastest animal is the cheetah. 6 The most dangerous roads are in India.

b Students' own answers.

5 a

	REVIEW
Name of book	*Brazzaville Beach*
Name of writer	William Boyd
Nationality of writer	British
Date of writing	1990
Type of book	thriller
Location (set in ...)	Africa
Time of story (which year)	second half of the 20th century
Main character	Hope Clearwater
Main event(s)	She notices that chimpanzees can be very violent.
Adjectives to describe book	exciting, interesting

b 7, 2, 5, 6, 1, 4, 3

6 a and b Students' own answers.

Lesson 3

1 a a [5] b [2] c [1] d [4] e [3]

b modern Russian sculpture [e]
The Marriage of Figaro [a]
abstract art [b] *Swan Lake* [d]

c 1 At the Hermitage Museum. 2 At the Smolny Institute. 3 Tickets for *Swan Lake* 4 At 11a.m. 5 On Wednesday.

2 1 b 2 a 3 a

3 1 b 2 b 3 c 4 c 5 b

4 1 Dario prefers traditional art to modern art. 2 The children prefer playing to reading. 3 I prefer action films to horror films. 4 Clara prefers watching television to listening to music. 5 We prefer going to concerts to visiting museums. 6 I prefer French food to Italian food.

5 1 I'll look at the map. 2 I'll check in my diary. 3 I'll get the key. 4 I'll ask him. 5 I'll phone the doctor. 6 I'll open the window. 7 I'll go to the supermarket.

6 1 I'll to get the instructions. B
2 I'll get it for you. C
3 I will 'll gave give you a refund. D
4 I'll turning on the lights. A

Review and consolidation 3

1 1 our house, ours 2 my wallet, mine 3 the pink flowers, ones 4 The bus on the right, one 5 the one with the blue door is their house, theirs 6 it's your bag, yours

2 1 Did, see 2 spent 3 left 4 had 5 bought 6 didn't keep

3 1 always, I always get up early. 2 usually, We usually go to the cinema on Friday evenings. 3 hardly ever, I hardly ever watch football. 4 never, I never drink coffee after 6 o'clock in the evening.

4 1 Dan and Gemma are making a Chinese meal. 2 What is Steve doing in the garden? 3 Laura is wearing a long skirt this evening. 4 What are you watching on TV? 5 Mum is not speaking to Dad at the moment. 6 The boys are playing tennis in the park. 7 Our daughter is sleeping in her room. 8 Where are you planning to go on holiday? 9 I am not having anything to eat. 10 What are you carrying in that bag?

5 1 usually work 2 don't get home 3 am having 4 am waiting 5 is coming 6 is bringing 7 enjoy 8 cook 9 are you doing

6 1 fast 2 noisily 3 healthily 4 well 5 casually 6 easily 7 quietly 8 comfortably 9 carefully 10 slowly

7 1 Mac is heavier than Ian. 2 Mac is older than Joe. 3 Mac is the tallest. 4 Joe is shorter than Mac. 5 Ian is the youngest. 6 Joe is heavier than Ian. 7 Joe is the shortest. 8 Ian is younger than Mac. 9 Joe is older than Ian. 10 Joe is the heaviest.

8 1 We prefer old films to modern films. 2 ✓ 3 Matt prefers playing football to playing badminton. 4 We prefer fish to meat for dinner. 5 She prefers opera to ballet. 6 Do you prefer swimming to sunbathing? 7 ✓ 8 I prefer doing roleplays to doing grammar exercises.

9 **a** 1 pretty 2 ballet 3 tight 4 pullover 5 slim 6 comedy 7 hot 8 belt

b 1 belt 2 hot 3 slim 4 ballet 5 pullover 6 comedy 7 tight 8 pretty

Unit 10

Lesson 1

1 **a** 1 underground train 2 flight 3 park 4 long-haul 5 bicycle

b 1 platform 2 park 3 Long-haul 4 bicycle 5 garage

2 **a** holiday rep

b and c
1 ✓ 2 ✓ 3 ✓ last winter 4 ✗ 5 ✓ 6 ✗ 7 ✓ last summer 8 ✓ when she was at university

3 Della's answers:
2 No, I haven't. 3 Yes, I've been to San Antonio, in Ibiza. Students' own answers.

4 **a** 1 been 2 went 3 Have 4 never 5 haven't 6 ever 7 went 8 been 9 haven't

5 1 I've been bungee jumping. 2 We haven't been to Bangkok. 3 Have you been to London? 4 Have they been on an package holiday? 5 John and Julie haven't been to Australia. 6 I haven't been on an adventure holiday. 7 Our parents have been to Florida. 8 Have you been to an

IMAX cinema? 9 We've been hiking in the mountains. 10 Have your cousins been to your new house?

6 1 d 2 f 3 b 4 c 5 g 6 a 7 e

7 2 Have you ever been to New York? 3 Have you ever been to a classical concert? 4 Have you ever been to a football match? 5 Have you ever been to Paris? 6 Have you ever been to an Internet café?
Student's own answers.

8 **a** A=/ə/   B=/ɪ/

b 1 /ə/ 2 /ə/ 3 /ɪ/ 4 /ə/ 5 /ɪ/ 6 /ə/

Lesson 2

1 1 water sports 2 cultural 3 beach 4 activity 5 sightseeing 6 winter sports

2 **a** 1 cultural 2 beach 3 skiing

b 1 Crete 2 Verona 3 Les Arcs

3 1 Verona, Crete, Les Arcs 2 Verona 3 Les Arcs 4 Crete 5 Les Arcs 6 Crete

4 1 Saskia hasn't cooked all her meals. 2 She's visited the sights. 3 Pawel has seen an opera. 4 He hasn't learnt to ski. 5 He has been on a city tour. 6 Karl and Tara haven't had a quiet week. 7 They've been to lots of nightclubs. 8 They've spent hours on the beach.

5 **a**

	INFINITIVE	PAST PARTICIPLE
1	become	become
2	catch	caught
3	drive	driven
4	forget	forgotten
5	keep	kept
6	meet	met
7	ride	ridden
8	wear	worn

b 1 Have you ever ridden ... 2 I've forgotten ... 3 I've never worn ... 4 Have you met ... 5 Gerald has caught ... 6 has become ... 7 has driven ... 8 Have your parents kept ...

6 **a and b**   1 b 2 b 3 a 4 b 5 a 6 b

7 **a and b**   Students' own answers.

Lesson 3

1 **a** C

b 1 petrol station 2 top speed 3 difficult 4 check 5 scooter 6 connect 7 great

c (possible answers:)
Advantages: You don't need to go to the petrol station. It's very cheap. Riding it is easy. It's easy to park. You don't need a driving licence. Adults or children can use it.
Disadvantages: It isn't very comfortable. It's quite heavy.

2 1 f 2 g 3 b 4 e 5 a 6 c 7 d

3 1 underground train 2 departure date 3 one-way ticket 4 economy class 5 rush hour

4 1 Watching horror films is scary. 2 Eating lots of fruit and vegetables is healthy. 3 Driving in fog is dangerous. 4 Learning a foreign language is difficult. 5 Swimming in warm water is relaxing. 6 Visiting new places is exciting. 7 Flying in business class is expensive.

5 1 Parking a car is difficult in big cities. 2 Getting information from the Internet is easy. 3 Sending flowers to your wife or girlfriend is romantic. 4 Getting an email from your best friend is nice. 5 Watching the news on TV is interesting.

6 **a** 1 tickets 2 to 3 way 4 economy 5 flight 6 stops

b b Return. We'd like to come back on Saturday the 28th.
c Economy class, please. d How much is that flight? e Is it a direct flight? f What time does it leave?

Unit 11

Lesson 1

1 **a** B

b 1 sharp objects 2 electronic devices 3 documents 4 luggage

c 1 d 2 c 3 e 4 a 5 b

2

	NECESSARY	NOT NECESSARY	POSSIBLE	NOT POSSIBLE
1		✓		
2	✓			
3	✓			
4			✓	
5				✓
6				✓
7	✓			
8		✓		
9	✓			
10				✓

3 1 You can't take drinks onto the plane. 2 You can't take food on the plane. 3 You have to be at check-in 2 hours before your departure time. 4 You have to turn off your mobile phone before you board the plane. 5 You have to wear your seat belt during the flight.

4 1 You can't drive a car when you are only 15 years old. 2 I can bring a friend to the party (if I want to). 3 We can't use our mobile phones in my office. 4 You have to show your receipt to the manager. 5 You can't park near the theatre. 6 Amanda doesn't have to pay because she's a member of the club. 7 You can pay by cash or credit card. 8 David and Lucy don't have to get visas to go to Canada.

5 1 traffic lights 2 offence 3 seat belt 4 driving licence 5 driving test 6 fine 7 obey 8 turn right

6 **a**
       /f/   /v/   /f/   /v/
You don't ha<u>v</u>e to ha<u>v</u>e a <u>F</u>rench <u>v</u>isa.

b 1 /f/ 2 /v/ 3 /v/ 4 /v/ 5 /f/

Lesson 2

1 1 an older English man, he didn't like school 2 an American woman in her thirties 3 a teacher of French and Spanish

2 **a** 1 2 2 1 3 1 4 3 5 2

b

	1	2	3
1 Age started school?	5	6	5
2 Location of school?	London	Texas	Scotland
3 Time spent at school?	9	12	13
4 Enjoyed school?	no	yes	yes
5 Favourite subject(s)?	sport	Maths & Geography	French & Spanish
6 Went to university?	no	started it	yes

3 **a and b** 2 Where did you go to school? 3 How long did you stay at school? 4 Did you enjoy school? 5 What was your favourite subject? 6 Did you go to university?

4 **a** 1 How many 2 Who 3 Where 4 What 5 How 6 When 7 Why

b 2 When did you start learning English? 3 Who do you live with? 4 How do you get to the school? 5 Which school did you go to? 6 What did you watch on TV yesterday? 7 Why are you learning English? 8 Which subjects did you do? Students' own answers.

5 **a and b** 1 ↘ 2 ↘ 3 ↗ 4 ↘ 5 ↗

6 **a, b and c** Students' own answers.

Lesson 3

1 **a** 1 No, she's catching the train home on Tuesday afternoon. 2 No, she's starting a day class/school on Wednesday. 3 Yes, she is. 4 No, she's taking her driving test on Friday afternoon. 5 No, she's going to a nightclub/Bailey's nightclub with Keira on Saturday. 6 Yes, she is.

b 1 Is she having the interview on Tuesday morning? Yes, she is. 2 What time is she catching the train on Tuesday? At 1.00. 3 When is she meeting the bank manager? At 2.00 on Thursday. 4 Is she going swimming with Dave on Friday? Yes, she is. 5 Is she going shopping on Saturday afternoon? No, on Saturday morning. 6 Who is Cristina going shopping with? Alison.

2 **a**

EDUCATIONAL INSTITUTIONS	QUALIFICATIONS	PEOPLE STUDYING	PEOPLE TEACHING	SCHOOL SUBJECTS
secondary school	degree	pupil	trainer	Physics

b Students' own answers.

3 1 optional 2 a vocational 3 part-time 4 state 5 distance-learning

4 ask about plans: What are you and Paula doing on Friday evening?; express an arrangement: We're taking Paula's niece to the cinema. suggest a time: Can you come at four o'clock?; refuse politely: I'm afraid we can't come then. suggest an alternative: Why don't you come to us on Saturday, then?; make an arrangement: Let's put it in our diaries.

5 **a** 1 I'm afraid we can't come then. 2 how about early Tuesday evening? 3 Let's say Tuesday evening at seven. 4 What are you and Paula doing on Friday evening? 5 We're taking Paula's niece to the cinema. 6 I'm afraid that's impossible. 7 Why don't you come to us on Saturday, then? 8 Let's meet in the pub for a quick drink first.

Unit 12

Lesson 1

1 1 coast 2 white-water rafting 3 canyon 4 island 5 sailing 6 trekking

2 **a** The photo shows Anthony and Belinda. The map shows where Anthony is going this summer.

b 4, 6, 7, 5, 2, 1, 3

c 1 cousins 2 trekking 3 drive 4 isn't 5 ten days

3 **a** 1 Are you going to 2 'm going to 3 're going to 4 're going to 5 're going to 6 'm going to 7 Is your girlfriend going to 8 's going to 9 're going to

4 1 I'm going to finish the course in September. 2 No, I'm going to send an email tomorrow. 3 This year they are going to stay with friends in Spain. 4 Henry is going to go sailing in Canada next year.   **5** She isn't going to study Science at university.   **6** But I'm going to study this weekend.

5 (possible answers)   **2** I'm going to lose weight/get fit.
3 We're going to get married.   **4** I'm going to get a job/be a computer programmer.   **5** We're going to buy a new TV.   **6** I'm going to go to/visit India.

6 a
2 He's <u>going</u> to fly to <u>Rome</u>.

b
1 We're <u>going</u> to buy a <u>car</u>.
2 I'm <u>going</u> to see the <u>doctor</u>.
3 She's <u>going</u> to meet my <u>parents</u>.
4 They're <u>going</u> to stay at <u>home</u>.
5 He's <u>going</u> to be a <u>painter</u>.

7   **1** later this year   **2** next week   **3** tomorrow   **4** the week after next   **5** In three years' time   **6** next year   **7** four years from now

Lesson 2

1   a   1 acting, singing, dancing, training   **2** session, election, competition   **3** producer, footballer, performer

b   people = 3   activities = 1   events = 2

2   a c

b   **1** D   **2** B   **3** C

c   1 He's an architect.   **2** in Boston   **3** because Richard only gets two weeks' holiday   **4** to get only two weeks' holiday   **5** in Milan   **6** No, it isn't.   **7** to be a web designer   **8** to learn all about web design   **9** to make (fantastic) websites   **10** to start their own web design company.

3   2 to send emails   **3** to get fit   **4** to commute to work **5** to visit our grandparents   **6** to lose weight

4   1 Jane flew to Berlin to visit her boyfriend.   **2** My son uses his computer to play games.   **3** I'm going to get an MP3 player to listen to music.   **4** We always go to the market to buy fresh food.   **5** My brother went to St. Petersburg to see the Hermitage Museum.

5   a   1 It was really interesting to hear all about your new office.   **2** I'm sorry you only get two weeks' holiday.
3 Things are fine here in Milan.   **4** Please write again soon and tell me all about your new colleagues!

b
1 I've, I'm, we're, It's, we've, that's   **2** really, quite   **3** exciting, part-time, local, fantastic, new, great, usual

6   a, b and c   Possible answer:
Dear Isabel
Thanks for your last letter. Congratulations on your new house! It was really interesting to hear about it. I'm very please that you're going to visit us here next summer.
Well, I have some news. Last week I started a new job. It's in .... I have to .... I'm really enjoying it. Next month I'm going to start a new (evening) class in .... at the sports centre, and tomorrow I'm going to buy a new mobile phone (because my old one is broken).
That's all my news. Write soon and tell me more about your new house.
Love
....

Lesson 3

1   a   become a politician, be a rock singer, go around the world, win a lot of money

b   2 travel around the world   **3** become a politician   **4** be a rock singer

2   1 to win   **2** doing nothing   **3** to travel   **4** flying   **5** to become   **6** to be   **7** to be   **8** playing   **9** singing

3   a   1 I wouldn't like working   **2** I really enjoy to do **3** I would like to becoming   **4** most of them like learn **5** I can't stand to take   **6** I really want start

b   1 I wouldn't like to work   **2** I really enjoy doing **3** I would like to become   **4** most of them like learning **5** I can't stand taking   **6** I really want to start

4   1 She would like to have a good music system because she likes listening to music.   **2** She would like to be a holiday rep because she likes visiting different countries.   **3** He would like to be a racing driver because he likes driving fast.
4 He would like to be a secondary school teacher because he likes helping young people.   **5** She would like to have lots of grandchildren because she likes being with children.

5   a and b

A /eɪ/	B /aɪ/
bake	bike
hate	height
day	die
aim	I'm
main	mine
late	light

6   a and b   Students' own answers.

Review and consolidation 4

1   1 ever, 've   **2** Has, went   **3** Have, have   **4** been, 's **5** Have, 've

2   1 I haven't spent a lot of money.   **2** Have you taken the driving test?   **3** Has she written any postcards?   **4** I haven't seen that film.   **5** The students haven't done their homework. **6** Have you ever played golf?   **7** Has Lena visited her parents? **8** We haven't gone on holiday this year.   **9** Henry hasn't bought a newspaper today.   **10** Have you had lunch?

3   1 ✗ <u>fly</u>, flying;   **2** ✗ are, is,   **3** ✓   **4** ✗ <u>pay</u>, paying;   **5** ✗ <u>are</u>, is;   **6** ✓

4   1 can't smoke in the college building.   **2** can smoke in the garden.   **3** can't bring food or drinks into the classrooms. **4** can get coffee and tea in the college café.   **5** have to show an identity card when they come into the college.   **6** can't use mobile phones during lessons.   **7** can use the computers in the library in the evenings.   **8** don't have to pay to use the computers.   **9** have to bring a pen and some paper to lessons.   **10** don't have to bring a dictionary.

5   1 are you doing, are taking   **2** Is Jane coming, 's driving **3** are your friends leaving, 're going   **4** are you cooking, 'm not cooking

6   1 're going to build   **2** 's going to do   **3** aren't going to buy   **4** 's going to buy   **5** 's going to get   **6** 're going to have **7** isn't going to get   **8** 'm going to buy   **9** Are you going to stay   **10** Are you going to visit

7   1 sunbathing, going   **2** 'd like   **3** playing, to be **4** gardening, wouldn't   **5** listening   **6** to come   **7** doesn't **8** to get   **9** going, can't

8   1 compulsory   **2** kindergarten   **3** tutor   **4** private **5** degree   **6** offence   **7** licence   **8** safety   **9** charity **10** continent

9   1 b   **2** g   **3** d   **4** c   **5** a   **6** h   **7** f   **8** e